ACTING ALONE

D1603663

ACTING ALONE

A Drama Teacher's Monologue

SURVIVAL KIT

DEMETRA HAJIDIACOS

J. GORDON SHILLINGFORD
PUBLISHING INC

Book design by Relish Design Studio
Author photo by Joel Ross
Printed and bound in Canada

We acknowledge the financial support of the Manitoba Arts Council, The Canada Council for the Arts and the Government of Canada through the Book Publishing Industry Development Program (BPIDP) for our publishing program.

J. Gordon Shillingford Publishing
P.O. Box 86, RPO Corydon Avenue
Winnipeg, MB
Canada   R3M 3S3

Library and Archives Canada Cataloguing in Publication

Hajidiacos, Demetra, 1975-

        Acting alone: a drama teacher's monologue survival kit / Demetra Hajidiacos.

Includes bibliographical references.

ISBN 1-897289-00-6

        1. Drama--Study and teaching (Secondary)   2. Theater--Study and teaching (Secondary).   I. Title.

PN2075.H34 2006   808.2'071'2   C2006-901014-5

For my loving husband Nick who encourages me,
my beautiful son Peter who sleeps sometimes
and my friend Jill wherever you are

*Every child is an artist. The problem is how to
remain an artist once we grow up.*

—Pablo Picasso

Acknowledgements

I would like to thank my mentor Kelly Daniels because had she not let me follow her around and hold her pencils for a number of years I would know next to nothing about teaching acting, directing and working with students; my husband Nick for his endless encouragement and support; my mom, Nikoletta Mattheos, for teaching me how to do ten things at once; Per Brask for being an inspirational playwriting teacher; Rory Runnells at the Manitoba Association of Playwrights for offering guidance and support on how to get started with this project; Jey Thibideau Silver for refusing to let me keep this idea in a drawer any longer; the Westwood Collegiate drama students for workshopping my monologues and offering extremely useful feedback; Sandy White for welcoming me into his classroom; all the theatre professionals who have brought their expertise into my classroom over the years fuelling my enthusiasm for teaching drama; all the theatre professors at the University of Winnipeg who have been model teachers to me and so many others; Gord Shillingford for believing in this book; and last but not least, my entire family including my wonderful parents and two brothers because if it weren't for my colourful upbringing I probably wouldn't have ended up in the theatre!

Table of Contents

INTRODUCTION

*Without art, the crudeness of reality
would make the world unbearable.*

—George Bernard Shaw

I've had countless conversations with colleagues over the years in regards to the lack of monologue material "out there" for young actors. Sure there are books and websites that offer monologue selections for young people, but they are few and far between and most are a compilation of monologues from plays that students have not even read.

No offence to the Bard himself, but how many times can we, as drama educators, sit back and enjoy hearing the following words uttered at general auditions for the school play or musical: *"O Romeo, Romeo! Wherefore art thou Romeo?"* And if it isn't that it's: *"But, soft! What light through yonder window breaks?"* And even more disheartening is *"I don't have a monologue. What's a monologue?"*

Personally, I've had my share of these arduously long auditions. I've seen students bring in poems from their English texts to recite and even a brave soul or two who has attempted to write his own monologue that has mercilessly ranged anywhere from 5 – 15 minutes in duration. I've seen pretty much every form of monologue disaster over the years and then some.

Conversely, I've seen students, provided with the right material, perform alone on stage with more finesse than I've seen on some professional stages. I've seen students write and perform their own material that has rivalled any monologues I, as their acting coach, could have ever mustered for them. And although I've directed dozens of major productions over the years including *Oklahoma!, Hello Dolly, Cabaret, Fame, Our Town, Romeo and Juliet* and *Oedipus Rex,* some of my most memorable teaching experiences have been writing and directing monologues for my students.

I fell in love with monologues while in university studying to be a teacher. I was cast in a brilliant play by Timothy Findley entitled *Can you see me yet?* In Findley's play, I played a catatonic woman who barely spoke until the end of the play where she delivers what I believe to be one of the most riveting monologues in Canadian theatre. I played the part of Rosemary, the young mother who murders her baby. Since then, either by coincidence or on purpose, I have had the pleasure of being cast to play women who delivered gripping monologues. As a result, I couldn't help but fall in love with the art of acting alone.

When I began teaching drama in the public school system, I endeavoured to teach students how to deliver monologues, using some techniques I had learned or invented along the way. Although I was enthusiastic to teach monologues, my long trips to the library and endless evenings of flipping through drama anthologies searching for monologues that were appropriate for students left me frustrated and often empty handed.

It wasn't until my fourth year of teaching that I decided to conquer this monologue deficit by teaching my students how to write their *own* monologues! When I began my after school "monologue club," I had 9 students interested in writing and performing their own pieces in an evening presentation for family and friends. From that time forward, teaching monologues became an indispensable component of my curriculum and our once tiny evenings of monologue presentations grew into packed house events featuring drama students from all four grade levels of high school performing in an evening entitled **Acting Alone.**

My students have won public speaking competitions, playwriting awards and performed on professional stages including Prairie Theatre Exchange's Mainstage during the Manitoba Drama Youth Festival and Manitoba Theatre Centre's Warehouse Theatre during the Manitoba Association of Playwrights' (MAP) annual high school playwriting competition. In addition to being confident writers and actors, as a result of participating in these evening monologue presentations, my students have learned to competently direct, stage manage and design costumes, sets, sound and lights.

As educators, we enjoy sharing information that makes lesson planning easier and more rewarding. We enjoy simplicity and learning new concepts that enhance our own material and make our unit plans richer and more fulfilling for our students. This book is based on my own experiences of teaching, writing and directing monologues for students. It is intended to educate you, the drama teacher looking for inspiration to incorporate monologues into your school's drama curriculum. You will learn how much fun it can be to write expressly for your students and teach them how to effortlessly write material for themselves.

I started writing this book because I found myself running out of material for my students. And if you're like me, you're running out of material as well. So let's face it, the only remedy for this is to A) Write for our students or B) Teach our students to write their own material. Implementing these two rewarding solutions into your already rich curriculum is precisely what this book will teach you to do!

In reading this book, you will unearth a whole new way of looking at monologues and their multiplicity of uses in your drama classroom. You will quickly discover how very easy it is to use monologues as a reference point to teach students acting basics, how to prepare for auditions and the art of acting alone on stage in front of an audience. Enjoy!

Chapter 1: **Why teach monologues to students?**

Performing a monologue is the most difficult thing an actor has to do because it's like playing goalie with no one shooting pucks at you.

—Blake Taylor

If you don't already teach monologues to your students, there are many reasons to get started right away. Here is a condensed list of promising uses that will be discussed in more detail in subsequent chapters:

- Preparing students for auditions
- Teaching students acting basics
- Teaching students to act truthfully or **realism** (acting that mirrors real life)
- Teaching students to direct
- Teaching students to write
- Teaching students to develop characters
- Teaching students to be comfortable on stage alone.

You'll notice that apart from the first and last points on the list, the remaining points can be covered just as well in a unit devoted to scene work, improvisation, or collective creations. So why are the first and last points on the list the dealmakers when considering whether or not you should teach monologues to your students? If you've ever directed a musical with 50 chorus members standing on stage with very little to do, as you race around telling one to blow kisses and the other to sweep the floor, you'll know how imperative it is to teach students to take care of themselves on stage when no one is delivering lines to them.

When I was studying acting at the University of Winnipeg, one of my instructors, Blake Taylor, put it best. Performing a monologue, he told us, is the most difficult thing an actor has to do because it's like playing goalie with no one shooting pucks at you. How true! When we act in a scene with a partner, our job as actors is to react to what our partner is throwing our way, whether it's words, lack of words or body language. Even students with no acting training are able to understand the very crux of acting after being told this plainly obvious pointer. And yet seasoned acting students can be left to feel inadequate standing on stage alone with no one giving them anything to react to.

When we teach students that acting is about responding, we don't teach them what to do in circumstances where there is nothing to respond to. As acting coaches, we teach students to be real, to act in the moment, to wait for something to happen before they move an arm hair. But what happens when an actor is alone on stage and his only acting partner is his cowering shadow?

Students who are trained to act alone are students who are skilled at filling in the blanks on stage, always finding something to do that will contribute to the story or the development of their character. These are students who smile when entering an audition room because they know they are prepared to show their best work. When something goes awry on stage they are able to steer the scene to safety. These are students who understand character development and are able to apply their concepts to any role including those created in the spur of the moment during an improvised scene. But above all, these are students who own the stage they walk on, exuding confidence to the rafters and beyond.

After reading this book, you may choose to create a small unit devoted to monologue work in order to simply prepare your students for audition situations or you may choose to use monologues to teach several units on character development, movement, voice, acting, writing and directing.

The choice is yours. But I do believe that you will find enough in the pages of this book to decide where monologue work can appropriately be used in your classroom. And because I know first hand that teachers are busy people, I've tried to make this book as user-friendly as possible. At the end of each chapter you will find a **Survival Kit** that gives you a concise summary of the important points covered in that chapter. While lesson planning, you can refer back to the **Survival Kit** for inspiration or even make it your 'to do' list for the unit. So why not get started!

Chapter 2: **Acting alone... not really!**

Generality is the enemy to all art.

—Constantine Stanislavski as quoted in
A Practical Handbook for the Actor

As discussed in chapter 1, performing a monologue is the most difficult thing an actor has to do. Therefore, I wouldn't recommend that you begin the school year with a unit on monologues. I *would* suggest, however, that you first introduce your students to some basic acting principles and give them the opportunity to perform scripted and improvised scenes with partners.

While this chapter will provide you with some basic information on acting, I suggest that you consider acquainting yourself with some acting theorists in the field. There are thousands of books on acting theory and practice available today. It's easy to get confused about which ones are worth the read and which ones will have a long life collecting dust in the school library. While I certainly haven't read every book on acting, I have come across some very good ones. Here is a list of recommended texts for your drama shelf that I know you will find useful:

- *A Practical Handbook for the Actor* by Melissa Bruder et al.: This book was written by students of David Mamet at the University of New York. It's less than 90 pages and includes explanations to useful terms like *literal* and *essential actions.* This is an excellent beginner book for students new to acting theory. I highly recommend this book as a classroom text for grade 9 students or students learning about acting for the first time. This book is so easy to read that aside from using it as my grade 9 classroom text, I also use it as a quick review in grades 10 – 12.

- *Sanford Meisner on Acting* by Sanford Meisner and Dennis Longwell: The late Sanford Meisner was a renowned acting teacher who taught at the Neighborhood Playhouse for fifty years and trained the likes of Dustin Hoffman and Robert

Duvall. The book is told in a narrative style, following Meisner as he trains a group of young actors to live truthfully under imaginary circumstances. The exercises in this book are provoking and challenging yet can be easily implemented in your classroom. This book is ideal for an advanced performance class. You may, however, also consider using some of Meisner's simpler exercises to teach basic techniques to your beginner classes. I use this book as my grade 12 student text. There's also a very good documentary that shows Meisner in action at the Playhouse entitled *The Theater's Best Kept Secret* (1985).

- *Truth in Comedy: The Manual of Improvisation* by Charna Halpern, Del Close and Kim Johnson: This book, based on the teachings of improv guru Del Close, demystifies comic improvisation. The book contains testimonials from funny men Chris Farley and Mike Myers and gives real examples from Second City performances and the Improv Olympics. You must possess a copy of this book if you are planning to teach improv or comedy to your students. My copy is dog-eared.

- *Acting with Style* by John Harrop and Sabin R. Epstein: This is a comprehensive text that explores the history, theory and practice behind the theatre's most celebrated genres including: Greek, Shakespeare, realism and the absurd. This text is a great reference when teaching a unit on a specific genre or directing a period piece.

- *Stages: Creative Ideas for Teaching Drama* by Talia Pura: This is a goody bag of activities for the drama teacher that covers everything from warm-up exercises to performance ideas. In addition to a comprehensive list of classroom exercises categorized by subject (voice, tableaux, improv, etc.) Pura shows teachers how to design units and even entire curriculums. This is a great book to keep on your desk.

- *True and False* by David Mamet: This book contains some of the same teachings that are found in the book written by his pupils (*A Practical Handbook for the Actor*) but really it serves as a kick in the pants to anyone who is considering pursuing acting as a career. The chapters in this book are short and to the point containing Mamet's no-nonsense approach to acting. I do not recommend this as a text for students...Mamet would make a grown man cry. This is however a great book for teachers to read. Be prepared; he unapologetically criticizes acting teachers, but for good reason!

- *The Poetics* by Aristotle: You **must** read the *Poetics* if you teach theatre. There is no getting around this one. If you don't want to read the entire thing, there is a good excerpt in a book entitled *Eight Great Tragedies* edited by Sylvan Barnet et al. Whole or in part, this is an excellent place to start when seeking some basic understanding of how a story is put together. As far as storytelling is concerned, not much has changed since ancient Greece.

- *Dorothy Heathcote: Drama as a Learning Medium* by Betty Jane Wagner: If you just want to be inspired about teaching or grasp the genuine power of using drama in the classroom, read this book, which follows the Donald Trump of, drama, Dorothy Heathcote, as she takes students on enrapturing voyages using their imaginations as vehicles. I highly recommend this book to any teacher embarking on a career in the performing arts.

WARMING UP

Some drama teachers confuse drama games with warm-ups. Drama games serve as a valuable tool for encouraging exploration and creativity, but unless the game ties into a principle that is being covered in the lesson, it has no place in the lesson! Use your unit on comedic improv to go nuts and pull out every fun activity you have in your repertoire, leave a list of games on your desk for substitute teachers or play one on Friday as a treat, but **don't confuse drama games for warm-ups.** The main purpose of a warm-up is to focus students and allow them the opportunity to practice listening, responding and thinking on the spot. Too much unfocused activity during a warm-up leads to (you guessed it!) an unfocused class.

Expectations

Students should refrain from talking during warm-ups and use the time to flex their most valuable muscle...their brain! You need to be very firm on this point. Students talking or not participating in a warm-up should be asked to sit out and spoken to at an appropriate time. Any sabotaging of the warm-up puts the entire class at a disadvantage.

Discuss student behaviour expectations at the beginning of the school year and avoid verbal conflicts when a student is asked to sit out. Students treated with respect in front of their peers will usually appreciate the gesture and respond in kind.

If you teach in a school that uses drama classes as a dumping ground for disruptive students, advocate that this not be the case in your classroom. Students have to want to be in your class and if that's not the case, it will become virtually impossible to teach while you are being heckled or your classroom activities are being sabotaged due to disrespectful behaviour or excessive talking.

Ensemble Activities

Here are some warm-up activities that I originally learned while studying directing under the guidance of Kelly Daniels and I've since used on numerous occasions with students of all ages. These warm-up activities get students focused and ready to work. They can be used at the beginning of every class, as warm-ups for rehearsals or even as entire lessons on focus and concentration. These activities emphasise ensemble work, build class morale and teach students how to work well with others.

Name Calling / Ball Throw

Students stand in a circle facing in. One student starts by making eye contact with another student, calling out that person's name and then passing a soft hand-sized ball to that student. The student who has received the ball then passes it in the same way to another student and the pattern continues until all students have had several turns. Students need to focus on their intended recipient, making every effort to help them catch the ball. The object is to pass the ball safely back and forth without dropping it. This activity will start out slow, until students are warmed up, and then it should become quite fast while always remaining focused.

This activity can also be done using character names. Students pass the ball to one another using the ball to show how their character feels about another character. In this variation the activity doesn't speed up and students can walk up to an actor and hand them the ball rather than throwing the ball.

Teachable moment: Ask students to articulate the metaphor in this activity by using the following questions: *If this were a scene what does the ball represent? Why do you not want your partner to drop the ball? Why are you helping your partner catch the ball?*

Zip Zap Boing—With Sound Effects

Students stand in a circle facing in. One student starts by forming a gun with his hand or index finger and passing an imaginary bolt of lightning to another student in the circle yelling "Zip" if that person is directly beside him or "Zap" if that person is not directly beside him. If a student does not want to accept the Zip or Zap he can Boing by placing his hands in front of his chest and boomeranging the bolt back to the person who sent it or he can choose to accept the bolt and pass it to another student. The pattern continues until each student has had several turns. The only rule is that you can't Boing a Boing. This activity will start slow and pick up speed.

Zip Zap Boing—No Sound

When students have mastered the activity with sound, have them play the game with no sound but using only gestures. Students will need to be more obvious with their gestures now that there is no sound.

Zip Zap Boing—No Gestures

When students have mastered the activity with no sound, have them play the game with no gestures! Students will need to pass with their eyes. If the lighting is bad in your room you may need to tighten the circle a tad. A Boing can be represented by a student lowering his head.

Teachable moment: *What do we learn from passing to one another? How did it feel to have your pass rejected?*

Name Murderer—With Words

Students stand in a circle facing in. Person A walks towards Person B (across the circle) with her arms stretched out in a zombie pose. Person B randomly stares at someone (Person C) to save her. Person C calls Person B's name. I know, you need a map to figure this one out for the first time! (see figure 1 below) When A makes it over to B, B walks towards C and the cycle continues as C now stares at a new person. This activity is also slow moving at first but then should become quite rapid with students running from one spot to the next.

Figure 1

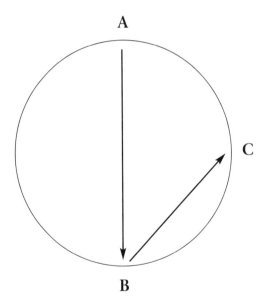

Name Murderer—No Words

Once students have mastered **Name Murderer** with words, repeat the activity with no words. This time C simply nods instead of calling B's name.

Teachable moment: *What did it feel like to be reliant on someone to save you? How is this activity similar to a scene?*

Twenty

Students stand in a circle facing in (see Figure 2). The best way to describe this activity is to explain to students that they are building a chain, one link at a time, by adding a number every time they get to the end of the chain. Each round of the activity only produces one new link while the rest of the students repeat the links that are already there.

Person A starts by saying "one." Person B (to Person A's right) then goes back to the beginning of the chain and repeats "one." Person C then adds another number to the link by saying "two." Person D starts at the beginning and says "one" again. The chain should sound like this:

A: **One**

B: One

C: **Two**

D: One

E: Two

F: **Three**

G: One

H: Two

I: Three

J: **Four**

K: One

L: Two

M: Three

N: Four

O: **Five**

Figure 2

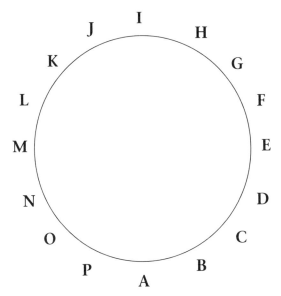

The people in bold add a link while the others merely repeat the links that are already there. Students should continue building the chain, always returning back to "one" after adding a new number, until they have reached twenty. If a student gets confused and says the wrong number (usually because he wasn't paying attention) the class has to start all over again from the beginning.

This activity takes an enormous amount of concentration. Encourage students to help one another by looking at the person to their right when they say their number and not simply calling out the number while staring at the floor. Another trick is to have the student at the end of the link punch his number so the next person knows he's "one" again. If students want to count with their fingers behind their back, that's fine as well.

Teachable moment: *Was it difficult to concentrate? Why? What made concentrating easier? What did it feel like to not know what you were supposed to say until it was your turn? What does this exercise teach us about being focused on stage?*

A WORD ON VOICE

If you don't have voice training, you could take a class at a local theatre or consider paying a professional to come in and teach a workshop on voice to your students. **When in doubt bring an artist out.** The investment is well worth it! Students need to be able to articulate and project on stage or everything else they do will be overshadowed by their lack of vocal training. While it may be fine to skip voice if your students are never going to see a stage because all your activities will be performed in your classroom, it really is doing students a disservice.

The following is a sequence of vocal exercises that I originally learned, while in university, from Gail Loadman. I've since used these exercises with students of all ages including adults, English students and debate teams.

All vocal exercises should be performed with students spread out facing into a circle and guided by you the teacher. You will demonstrate and your students will repeat. Even when students get the hang of an exercise, you still need to demonstrate before students jump in. This keeps the activity organized and free of confusing overlap.

Standing Tall

The first thing students need to do is learn how to stand tall. You will miraculously see teenage boys gain close to a foot in height after performing this simple trick! Have students stand with their feet directly under their hips. There should be a slight gap in between their feet but not a huge gap. Then have students take a small piece of hair from the top of their heads and pull as if they were a puppet.

Finding the diaphragm

The next thing students need to do is learn how to locate their diaphragm because all good voice control comes from a well supported diaphragm. Have students place their right or left hand (depending on preference), supported by the other, palm down on their belly button. Their belly button should be in the centre of the palm of their hand. Have students take deep breaths in through their nose and out through their mouth dramatically pushing their belly in and out on each inhale (out) and exhale (in).

Projection

With students' hands still on their diaphragms and feet planted under their hips, have them repeat the following:

1. Ha (diaphragm out) Ha (diaphragm in)
   Do the "Ha Ha" in different registers (high, middle, low)

   Make sure students are not using their vocal cords but that the sound is coming from their diaphragms. Have them project as much as possible. Allow students time to rest. When they rest have them take in deep breaths through their nose and out their mouth.

2. Pimlico, Pimlico
   Pumpkins and peas/
   Pepper them properly else you will sneeze/

   Pop in the pigskins, leave until one/
   Pimlico, Pimlico, then they'll be done

3. If you are rehearsing a play or scenes, have students repeat lines from the play with intensity.

4. Any declarative sentences. "What a beautiful day." "Get out of my house."

Projection Pyramid

Have students loosen their wrists and let their arms hang. Starting with the right arm, have students swing their wrists out as if they are throwing a Frisbee to the floor. Then repeat with the left hand. Each time students swing their wrists out they should say "Hey." Each time students fling their wrists they should also raise their arm a little, throwing the imaginary Frisbee higher and higher until both arms are high in the air above their bodies and students are on the tips of their toes throwing Frisbees to the ceiling. Every time students raise their arms higher, the "hey" should get louder. The loudest "hey" is at the top of the pyramid, at which point students should point their index fingers downwards and make with their hands as if they are descending a slide and say "Heeeeeey" all the way down. After demonstrating the initial "Hey, Hey" students can do the pyramid along with you.

Articulation

The following are a series of articulation exercises. First break sentences into fragments (breaks are signified by "/") and have students repeat each fragment, over-exaggerating each sound and opening their mouths fully. This should be done slowly and with emphasis on pronouncing each sound.

Then have students take a deep breath in through their nose and repeat the sentence 5 times, quickly, on one breath. Allow students time to rest in between each new sentence.

- A big black bug / bit a big black bear / made the big black bear bleed blood.

- Peter Piper picked a peck of pickled peppers /
  A peck of pickled peppers Peter Piper picked /
  If Peter Piper picked a peck of pickled pepers /
  Where is the peck of pickled peppers Peter Piper picked?

- Toy Boat

- Lemon Liniment

- Round and round the rugged rock / the ragged rascals ran.

- Six, sick, Swiss, wrist watches

- Will you wait for Winnie and Willie Williams in Winnipeg or Wawanesa?

  This one is slightly different in the break up

  Will you wait for Winnie /
  Will you wait for Winnie and Willie Williams /
  Will you wait for Winnie and Willie Williams in Winnipeg or Wawanesa/

Frisbee Wrists

Students should fling wrists outward as if throwing a Frisbee, alternating between right and left hands. Frisbees should be thrown at elbow height. Students will recite "Bree (right) Brae (left)" together with you after you have demonstrated the initial "Bree Brae." Start slow and then get faster and faster. Repeat the activity with the sounds "Broo Bro." Students should roll the "r" sound.

MOVEMENT

There are many great exercises involving mime that get students using their bodies to tell stories. Here are some basic ones that are fun and easy to do.

Where am I?

Have one student start by going up onto the stage area and miming being in a specific location (a park for example). When students figure out where the actor is they can slowly enter the scene either by interacting with others or doing something independently in that location. When all students are up, ask them where they are. If it wasn't clear, discuss why and try again.

Exploring themes through tableaux

There are many weighty themes that can be explored through movement and body language. Have students explore themes through a series of tableaux (still pictures). Divide the class into groups or do the tableaux as a class. Ask students to go into the tableau one by one, taking time to see where they can add to the picture. Students do not have to be connected (i.e., time and place). One actor can be a homeless person in a park while another is an heiress on a yacht; the important thing is that every actor contributes to the theme of the tableau. If there is a place for one actor to connect with another (perhaps consoling someone who is crying), that also works well.

The following are examples of themes you can explore through tableaux.

1. Poverty

2. War

3. Philanthropy

4. Terrorism

5. Peace

Take a real picture of the tableau to show your class; have students view their pose in front of a mirror; or tap students out one by one so they can come out of the tableau to see what they have created collectively as a group. Use the tableau as a means of opening up a discussion about certain themes you would like to explore. I've never found tableaux useful in comedy.

Effort Actions

Using the following **Effort Actions** originally developed in 1960 by Rudolph Laban in his book *The Mastery of Movement* (chapter 3), allow students to explore with different "tempo-rhythms" (Harrop, Espstein, 195-196). The following table represents Laban's 8 Effort Actions.

Weight	Time	Focus in Space		Laban Effort Action
Strong	Quick	Direct	=	to Punch
Strong	Sustained	Direct	=	to Press
Gentle	Quick	Direct	=	to Dab
Gentle	Quick	Flexible	=	to Flick
Strong	Quick	Flexible	=	to Slash
Strong	Sustained	Flexible	=	to Wring
Gentle	Sustained	Flexible	=	to Float
Gentle	Sustained	Direct	=	to Glide

Have students move freely in the room changing their weight (strong/gentle or, if you prefer, heavy/light), direction (direct/flexible or, if you prefer, direct/indirect) and speed (quick/sustained or, if you prefer, quick/slow) on your command. For instance, tell them to walk lightly, as though they weigh nothing and then heavily, as though they weigh one ton. Have them move quickly, then very slowly. Have students move in a straight line (direct) and then indirectly (flexible). Combine speeds, weights and directions to arrive at the terms above: **Glider, Presser, Dabber,** etc. When you begin scene and monologue work with your students, ask them what their character's Effort Action is. The captain of the volleyball team may be a **Puncher** while the dropout junky may be a **Floater.**

There is a useful instructional video entitled *Laban for Actors: The 8 Effort Actions* (1997) that shows theatre instructor Blake Taylor, of the University of Winnipeg, instructing students on how to use Laban's technique.

Centres

When I was first taught about centres I had a hard time taking the bus or watching strangers walk by in the mall. It became humorously apparent that everyone, no matter how subtly, has a centre or two. Your students will be coming to you days later telling you they laughed out loud when they realized their friends and family have centres too!

This is a very easy principle for students to wrap their heads around. Have students move freely in the room imagining their bodies are being pulled by a string that is attached to a specific body part. Call out the following body parts one at a time. When students demonstrate an understanding that they are being pulled by that part, go on to the next.

1. Nose

2. Chin

3. Ear

4. Forehead

5. Shoulders

6. Chest

7. Stomach

8. Hips

9. Knees

10. Index finger

Going through the list again have students imagine characters that lead with that particular body part. Characters who are led by their noses may be nosy people. Perhaps they use their nose to get into other people's business. An academic may be led by his chin, an eavesdropper by his ear, a soap actor by his forehead, a body builder by his shoulders, a cheerleader by her chest, a pregnant woman by her stomach, an Elvis impersonator by his hips, an old man by his knees and a small child by his index finger. Offer suggestions of who they might be but allow students to also come up with their own original ideas. As students create characters and wander around the room, side coach them with lines like *"Everything you do is about your ear; when you see people it's through your ear; when you turn, your ear turns first; your ear is the most noticeable part of your body."*

AND ACTION!

Like most high school teachers, I started out teaching junior high, where I learned a thing or two about **realism!** Kids that age, much to our chagrin, are constantly physically doing things to one another. In junior high, it's commonplace to see a snickering student pinch an unsuspecting victim in the arm, causing him to jump out of his seat screaming in pain. What this snickering junior high student has done is an **action**. He's done something (pinched his neighbour) because he wanted something (to get him to scream out loud in the middle of a test).

Acting, not any different from junior high, is all about doing things to other people to get a reward. It is the actor's job to determine what he wants from his scene partner. Here are some examples of clear actions that an actor may play on stage:

■ I want my lab partner to ask me out on a date.

■ I want my boss to give me a raise.

■ I want my brother to lend me his car.

The best way to introduce students to actions is to allow them the opportunity to practice through exercises/warm-up activities, two-person improvised scenes, two-person scripted scenes and finally monologues.

Action Exercise

This is an excellent acting exercise that I originally learned from Jey Thibideau Silver, PTE's educational director, and I have since refined and broken into three parts. This exercise can be used in your first lesson of the year or as a refresher lesson when students need a reminder of what they are supposed to be doing on stage…performing actions!

Part 1—Acting without words

Divide your class into pairs. Have partners face each other making room for themselves (at least 3 arms' lengths from any other pair). Have students decide who is 'A' and who is 'B'. Explain to students that you will call out actions and they will perform those actions to their partners in mime (without words). Students will continue to perform their action until you call out a new one.

Announce the following sequence in a clear monotone voice remembering to say the letter 'A' or 'B' before each action. Your instructions should sound like "A) Ignore…B) Teach…" Allow for about 5 seconds between announcing new actions so students have time to perform their action but not enough time to think before they act. Notice all actions are action verbs!!! Any action verb can be an action. **Anything an actor can physically do to another actor is an action.**

A	Beg
B	Help
A	Reject
B	Beg
A	Give
B	Take
A	Threaten
B	Bribe

A	Ignore
B	Teach
A	Hurt
B	Forgive
A	Mock
B	Mock
A	Hide
B	Seek
A	Irritate
B	Ignore
A	Accuse
B	Deny

Repeat the sequence asking students to switch places with one another. Students who were 'A' will now be 'B' and vice versa. Feel free to create your own original sequence or have students quickly jot down a list of 10 actions that you can collect in a hat and pull out during warm-ups.

Part 2—Acting with words

Repeat Part A but this time, have students verbalize their actions using improvised dialogue.

Part 3—Action Reaction

Simply call out one action "A) Take" and have students react to one another, creating their own sequence as a result of that one initial action. Part 3 can be done without words and then with words.

THE WHO, WHAT, WHERE OF THEATRE

A great way to get students started on working with **clear** and **easy** actions is to have them perform two-person improvised scenes containing a Who, a What and a Where.

Improvised Scenes

It's very, very easy to set up a basic **Who, What, Where** improv for your students. Select two volunteers and ask the class to offer up the following information:

- **WHO** are we? What is our relationship?
  Examples: siblings, classmates, co-workers, spouses

If you are doing a unit on realism, students should only play characters that are their own age and gender. For fun improv, that's not necessary.

- **WHAT** does person A want from person B? What is the initial action?
  Examples: Person A wants _____ from person B
  Person A wants forgiveness, revenge, praise, a favour, etc.

  I find that the fill-in-the-blank approach works best because it forces students to articulate their action in one word and avoids playwriting. "Forgiveness" is pretty open and allows the actor to make his own choices. Any more information from the class limits what the actor can create himself on stage.

- **WHERE** does the scene take place?
  Examples: A coffee shop, the school cafeteria, on a bus

Since it's A's job to hit B up for something, the location should be somewhere where B is not a flight risk. His place of employment, waiting for an important interview or while A is driving him somewhere are all good suggestions.

I like to write the **WHO, WHAT, WHERE** on the white board so we can work through the set-up as a group and refer to it throughout the scene.

I use improv as my first unit of the school year with every grade level no matter how novice or experienced. I side coach through the scenes until students have truly mastered putting an improvised scene together with a beginning, middle and end (remember when I said read *The Poetics!*). I later grade their final improvised scene to cap the unit.

STORY STRUCTURE: BEGINNING, MIDDLE & END

All scenes and monologues are stories. So it's important that acting students understand the basics of **story structure**. All stories have a beginning, middle and end. The beginning is when the **initial action** is introduced (the problem). The middle is the **climax** and the end is the **resolution**.

I started drawing the following diagram on chalk boards (figure 2) when I taught grade 7 language arts and have used it with drama classes of all ages ever since. I ask students to picture a balloon (character or characters). The balloon without air is nothing. When we begin to blow air (problems) into the balloon we have the beginnings of a story. When we fill the balloon until it can't hold anything more it explodes (climax). After the balloon has exploded we are left with pieces that can be cleaned up or left scattered on the floor, whichever, the important thing is that the pieces can never be put back together again in the same way. It's that simple!

Figure 2

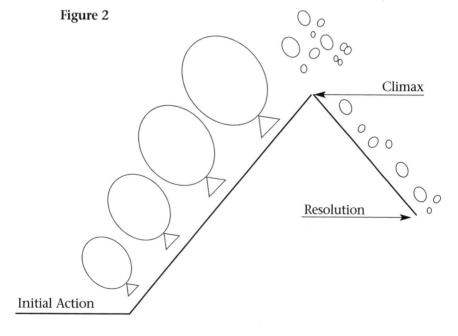

Climax

Resolution

Initial Action

IMPROV RULES!

High school students love improv. And it's a good thing too since it's absolutely imperative that your students are able to improvise. I can't think of a better way to start the school year than with a unit on improv. When you move on to scripted scene work and eventually monologue work (we'll get there, don't worry!) you'll be happy you spent the time teaching your students how to improvise and consequently, how to build a scene. Here are some tips to get you started:

1. **The One Big Lie** (Wagner, 67): Dorothy Heathcote so brilliantly coined this phrase and it means exactly what it implies. Theatre is merely an imitation of real life happenings. In order for an improv to appear real, the actors involved have to believe in the circumstances. A major barrier in improvisation is when one actor blocks her partner's ideas. This happens when one actor says, "Well, you should know what he's like, you've known Bob for three years" and the other actor replies, "Who's Bob?" Then a big argument erupts over whether or not this person really knows Bob. This is called **blocking** and it essentially kills the scene. To avoid blocking another actor's ideas and putting the scene to a halt, remember this rule: **When someone throws a fact into the imaginary circumstances of the scene it becomes a truth.** If your partner says you broke mom's heirloom vase, you did. If he says you pick your nose and eat it during math, you do that too.

2. The audience simply gives a suggestion to start the scene (Person A wants $50.00 from person B). That suggestion might only take the actors as far as the first 20 seconds of the scene. Since every scene should really be about the relationship between the people in the scene, the initial action or suggestion offered by the audience will get the ball rolling but should not be the entire scene. Person B can reply to A's request for money by saying, "Stop asking me to give you things!" and the third line in the scene could have absolutely nothing to do with the $50.00: "Well, I wish I had a job like you and then I wouldn't have to beg for money!" In a scene

there are several actions or **beats**. When an actor changes his action from "making person B feel sorry for me" to "lashing out at person B" a **beat change** has occurred. In a scene there are many beat changes which help to move the scene along.

3. Students should use the first 15 seconds of the scene to establish the **WHERE**. Through mime or the use of simple props, the actors need to let the audience know where they are. The rule is: **There should be no dialogue in the first 15 seconds of the scene.**

4. After the **where** has been established, Person A needs to get to the goods right away and deliver his **WHAT**. His first sentence should be something like "So I was wondering, can I have the car tonight?" If students do not get to the goods in the first sentence, stop them and make them start the scene again. No one wants to listen to "Hi how are you," "Good thanks" at the beginning of every scene! Most improvisers know to start the scene in the middle. This is just a simpler way of getting there with students.

5. The audience should be able to pick up from the first couple of lines in the scene the **WHO**. It's A's job to make it evident with his first line that he's a little brother grovelling for the car. The audience doesn't need fairly obvious hints like "Hey big brother, can I have the car tonight?" to help us determine the relationship. Explain to students that there is also no need to discuss their relationship in great detail reminiscing about their childhood. This may occur when a student begins a line with "remember the time when we...." Any defining of the relationship in words rather than actions is called **exposition** and has no place in a scene of any kind, unscripted or otherwise. Forget about the past. Direct students to keep things in the now. What is happening in *this* moment?

6. A scene is like a ping pong match. Provided your partner is hitting the ball back to you, you're still playing. If your partner keeps dropping the ball or refusing to pass, you're not playing much of a game. The ideal improv, like the ideal ping pong match, is when your partner tries to hit everything you

throw at them and vice versa. Acting is a series of actions and reactions. One person can not carry a two-person scene...only a one-person scene (we're almost there!).

7. All good things must come to an end and there's nothing worse than a scene that doesn't end. And since A has the job of starting the scene with the **WHAT**, it's only fair that B should mark the end with his departure. A good example would be "Thanks for the car man, you won't regret this."

I'LL HAVE MY STAKE WELL DONE

When I studied playwriting at the University of Winnipeg, my professor, Per Brask, told our class something that stuck with me and has altered the way I teach my students to analyze characters' motivations. He said that all characters, just like real people, do things because deep down they think that what they are doing will make them happy. Eureka! So in fact, the hostess with the mostess believes that her guests' praise will make her happy; the brown-noser at work thinks that the boss's approval will make him happy; and the mother who hovers over her children day and night feels that the only thing that will make her happy is her children's undying affection.

Nothing an actor does on stage is insignificant. Everything he does is because he wants to gain something for himself. If an actor wants an ex to go away he should really want her to go away; if he wants his co-worker to go out on a date with him, he should really want that date. The **stakes** should always be sky high. And students should understand that it's not their sanity or pride that's really at stake, but even more importantly, their happiness!

Make students work hard for what they want. I tell mine that if they're not breaking a sweat, they're not working hard enough. If a student's action looks weak, make him do it over and over again until he categorically demonstrates that he can not live without whatever it is he is striving to attain. Be firm. Do not allow students to continue in a scene if it looks like they don't understand why they are doing what they are doing. Take the scene one line at a time. It may take an entire class to master a single beat of a scene but that time will have been well spent. Acting is hard work. The sooner your students learn this, the sooner they will respect the craft and strive for perfection in everything they do.

LISTEN, ACCEPT AND CHOOSE

Acting teachers are constantly reminding students not to anticipate their partner's actions. We see it all the time when an eager young actor thinks he is saving a scene by reacting when there is nothing to react to. As teachers, we want our students to understand that acting is about playing with others and there is no need to manufacture artificial reactions where none are necessary.

One of the best things you can do as a drama educator is to bring in artists from the community to teach workshops to your classes. I've brought in directors, actors, storytellers, improvisers, designers, playwrights, stage managers, filmmakers; anyone really who will enhance my units and give students some inspirational stories from "the business."

When I began coaching improv, I brought in the funniest comedy troupe in town, The Spleen Jockeys, to teach my team a thing or two about building a scene from scratch. While we learned many invaluable lessons from these funny folk, the most important lesson was that scenes are built on the backs of actors and there is no place for anticipation when you have no idea what is coming next!

The Spleen Jockeys taught my students that there are three simple rules to improvisation:

1. **LISTEN** to what your partner is giving you (verbal or nonverbal).

   Your partner announces "I am the Queen of England."

2. **ACCEPT** what you are hearing to be the truth and nothing but the truth.

   You need to take a moment to acknowledge what you've just heard.

3. **CHOOSE** what you're going to do about it.

Your character responds, "It's time for your medication, Mrs. Johnson."

I have since taken these three rules and applied them when directing scripted scenes, and in particular monologue work. Often students feel rushed to get their lines out when it's their turn to speak not even listening to what their partner has told them. This is called **tailgating**. Mostly students do this out of nervousness and in a rehearsal situation I'll make them go back and **listen**, **accept** and **choose** before they deliver anything, verbal or nonverbal, to their partner.

SILENCE!

There is a universal misunderstanding among students that acting is talking. Acting is not about talking, acting is about doing. Sometimes we do with words, sometimes we do with looks, and sometimes we do by doing very little at all.

Try having your students perform improvised scenes with no words. Go back to the **Action Exercise** and do it without words. Train students to look at each other and react to one another. The sooner they become aware that all their attention should be placed on their partner, the sooner they will forget their stage fright and lose themselves in the moment. And that's what we want. Moment-to-moment acting that is based on what is happening in the now and not some preconceived notion of how a scene should look.

STATUS

Just like in real life, characters face the reality of living in a society where there is always someone richer, smarter and better looking. High school students inherently understand status. Their status usually involves friends, cars and curfews. Whether it's material possessions or personal qualities, students need to be able to identify who is a winner and who is a loser by societal standards. There are some tremendously meaningful discussions that can arise from this subject and we, as teachers, should take those teachable moments whenever we find them. The following exercise can be used to instigate dialogue about pressing social issues. This exercise is also a great lead into monologue work (finally!).

Status Exercise

Hand out coloured scarves to half the class and label them using present day stigmas (e.g.: being homeless). Instruct students who are not wearing scarves to interact with the "labelled" students making direct eye contact. Conversely, instruct those wearing scarves to avoid contact with others. Go through several scenarios and allow students to be both the "labelled" and the "labeller." After the activity, have a circle discussion about this phenomenon in our society. What if anything do we do to perpetuate this "labelling"? What can we do to stop this? Are there students in their school who might feel "labelled"?

AND FINALLY...MONOLOGUES

As drama teachers, we generally design our curriculums using similar frameworks. We begin with teaching students some warm-up and ensemble activities; then we teach students how to use their bodies through a series of movement exercises; we teach them how to articulate and how to project their voices using their diaphragms; we teach them how to execute **actions**, maybe a little of the Bard, a field trip to a professional show, some scene work, a little improv and before you know it it's June already.

So where do monologues fit in? Monologues *should* fit in right after students have learned the acting basics already outlined in this chapter and after completing a unit on scene work. **Until students understand what it's like to act truthfully with a partner, they will not be ready to learn how to act without a partner.** The following chapters will touch upon three different kinds of monologues: original monologues written by students (chapter 3), original monologues written by teachers for their students (chapter 4), and scripted monologues that are stand-alone pieces (chapter 5).

ACTING ALONE

To gain a better understanding of what a monologue is, let's take a look at the origins of the word. In Greek, mono means "alone" and *logos* means "speech." The word *monologos* means a one-person speech.

That seems fairly obvious, I'm sure, even to those who don't speak Greek. But you might be interested in knowing that in Greek, the word "monologue" is also a verb, monologo, which means "speaking alone."

So what does this add to our understanding of performing monologues? Simple; while there is a person B, in most monologues he doesn't speak! And because he doesn't speak, the actor performing the monologue doesn't have to create fake reactions to an imaginary person's responses. It's like person A is delivering a long bit of dialogue in the context of a greater scene (remember the improvisers who start in the middle?).

It's difficult watching someone deliver a monologue in which their imaginary scene partner is talking to them. It looks ridiculous and really only works in one of two scenarios: 1) a comedic scene where God is talking to the actor or 2) the actor on stage hears voices that no one else hears because he's insane! As an audience, we have the ability to suspend disbelief, but those limits do not include seeing invisible scene partners. If more than one person in the scene is talking, real or not, the definition of "monologue" does not apply to that piece.

So what do we need to know about acting alone on stage that differs from performing in a two-person scene? Here's a primer that will be discussed in more detail in the chapters to come.

An actor performing a monologue should:

1. Place person B out in the audience but never make eye contact with the audience unless the monologue is directed at them as is the case in a public speech. The actor should choose a very specific location for person B. Person B should always be stationary and not move around. A grounded person B helps person A create a more intimate and intense

exchange. When possible, person B should be placed over the heads of the audience. Have students pick a fixture at the back of the theatre as their guide (the window of the tech booth, the clock or the door). This helps students build that ever important **fourth wall** between them and the audience. Creating a fourth wall basically means filtering out the audience so an actor can focus on his imaginary circumstances.

2. Sit or stand. Should not pace. Should not sit and stand but sit or stand. This again helps students focus their energy creating a more intense exchange.

3. Clearly establish the **where** in the first two seconds of the scene through speech or display (costume is the best giveaway if the actor's first line does not reveal the **who, what, where**). An actor clad in an apron and hair net immediately transports us to a restaurant's kitchen.

4. Have no more than one prop.

5. Use a mime box or chair for sitting but no other furniture. An actor performing a monologue should be able to carry everything he needs for his piece in one trip.

6. Be as far downstage as possible.

7. In a performance situation be illuminated in a tight pool of light that covers only the area he is occupying and not any other surrounding area.

8. **Never** be interrupted by Person B.

9. Be sweet and to the point. A monologue should be no longer than 2 minutes. Student monologues should ideally be 1 minute long.

10. Play specific **actions**, have clean **beat changes** and high **stakes**.

And of course, have fun!

THE ACTING SURVIVAL KIT

- Read theorists on acting
- Drama games are not warm-ups!
- Actors need to learn how to articulate and project using their diaphragms.
- Actors should know their **centres.**
- Actors should know if they **punch, press, dab, flick, slash, wring, float or glide.**
- What an actor does to another actor is his **action.** Actions are action verbs and should be articulated in one word: beg, accuse, take, deny.
- All scenes should have a **who, what, where.**
- All scenes should have a **beginning** (initial action), **middle** (climax) and **end** (resolution).
- Use improv to teach students acting basics. A good improv:

  1. Has no **blocking.**

  2. Has several **beat changes.**

  3. Establishes the Who, What, Where in the first 20 seconds of the scene.

  4. Has no **exposition.**

  5. Is like a ping pong match.

  6. Should end.

- Actors should always have high **stakes** because their character's happiness is at stake.
- **Listen, Accept** and **Choose.**
- Silence!
- Actors should know their character's status or place.

- When acting alone, person B should be quiet and still!
- When performing a monologue actors should:

1. Know where B is.
2. Be stationary.
3. Clearly establish the who, what and where.
4. Have no more than one prop.
5. Use only a chair or mime box for furniture.
6. Be as far downstage as possible.
7. Be in a tight light.
8. Never be interrupted by Person B.
9. Be short and to the point.
10. Play specific actions, have clean beat changes and high stakes.

Chapter 3: Tricking students into writing, editing and directing

Everything that has happened before me I have something in common with, and this is my secret for finding material for drama.

—Dorothy Heathcote as quoted by Betty Jane Wagner
in her book *Drama as a Learning Medium*

If you've just flipped to this chapter hoping to gain information about getting students started on writing, I recommend you go back and read chapters 1 and 2 first. In those chapters you will find some excellent tools that will help lead students into writing.

This chapter isn't going to teach you typical "writing" exercises involving writing non-stop for five minutes or brainstorming ideas. Nor will it teach you to use a tree, map or web to elicit creative ideas from students. If you've ever tried to write anything this way you'll know these exercises don't work. I also find drama exercises that involve feeling around in space for something that isn't there confusing and unproductive. In fact, don't even tell students that they'll be "writing" because for the most part they won't!

The writing exercises you will find in this chapter are devised for actors, not writers. Students rarely sign up for drama to participate in the writing component; however, if you can trick them into it, they themselves will be amazed at how fun and easy creative writing can be!

CREATING A SPACE CONDUCIVE TO LEARNING

If you don't have a stage in your classroom create one by using tape on the floor or simply facing all the chairs or mime boxes in the room to one end of the classroom. Make sure that the stage area is **completely** bare (no costume racks or set pieces from old musicals). Only set pieces being used by the actors should be on the stage at any given time.

De-clutter your classroom and give students the opportunity to move and breathe without feeling they're working in a storage closet (something many drama classrooms become during production time). I can't be more frank about this: clutter is death to creativity. Fight tooth and nail to ensure your classroom is not being used to house old set pieces and costumes. Tell your administration to set aside a room in the basement for your costumes and sets and if that isn't being done, store them in the hallway outside of your classroom until it is. No one is storing old science tables and stools in the physics lab, so why should the drama room be a dumping ground? If there's *really* no place you can store old sets, donate them or have students carry them to the curb! The only thing students need in a drama room is a place to sit.

Insist that students don't bring a lot of stuff with them to class but what they do bring, backpacks and jackets, should be piled in an unused corner of the room. Create a big sign pointing to where backpacks should be placed. Also insist that students stack chairs and mime boxes along one wall of the room at the end of every class. An organized space will help students focus and give them room to explore.

DEVELOPING CHARACTERS

Writers intuitively base their characters on real people. Even better are those who base their characters on real people who they know on some intimate level.

Because I dislike traditional writing exercises, the exercises you'll find here are referred to as **non-writing exercises.** Your students will appreciate your anti-writing approach and you'll appreciate the fact that the exercises found here are student led and require no prepping from your end!

NON-WRITING EXERCISE #1—PEOPLE WATCHING

I was first introduced to this exercise while rehearsing a Brecht play directed by Kelly Daniels. When I realised its potential as a writing exercise for my students and, even better, a way to get students to write their own monologues, I was thrilled.

Part A—Show and Tell Homework

Again, it is *very* important that you do not tell students that they will be writing. Call this a character exercise or tell students this is a continuation of their acting unit (which it is).

Students need to observe someone who they think is interesting in some way. This exercise doesn't work if the subject knows he is being analysed. Students may select to observe anyone from a complete stranger to a family member living in the same house as them. The important thing is that they identify a person that strikes them as being interesting for whatever reason.

Part B—Show and Tell

One by one have students "show" the person they observed on the stage area without using words. Have students mime out the sequence of events that they observed this person do. Insist students make their presentations short but don't give them a specific time limit. If the presentation is dragging on too long and the group has gotten the gist of the situation, ask the actor to start wrapping it up but don't stop the presentation abruptly.

After each student's presentation, ask them who they saw—avoiding names if the person is someone known to the class—and what struck them as interesting about that person. Then thank the student and move on to the next.

After everyone in the class has presented, engage students in a circle discussion about the activity. What was interesting about the activity? What did they learn by observing others?

Cap the lesson by informing students that what they just participated in was the first step in character development. By showing us an interesting person on stage, they created the beginnings of a character.

NON-WRITING EXERCISE #2—TELLING A STORY

This exercise is my retaliation against all those "character sheets" I've filled out over the years. Tell students that in the following exercise they will become the character they observed in Exercise #1.

Part A—Visualisation

Have students spread out in comfortable positions around the room. Tell students to close their eyes as you guide them through a series of questions for them to think about. Allowing students time to internalize each question, ask students the following:

1. I want you to go back to that place that you were observed in. Look around and see where you are. What are you doing there?

2. Why are you there?

3. Do you want to be there?

4. Who else is there?

5. If you're alone, does that bother you?

6. If you're surrounded by people, does that bother you?

7. How are you feeling today? Was it a good day, a bad day?

8. Are you in a hurry to be somewhere or are you quite content with where you are?

9. Is there something eating at you today?

10. What's eating at you?

Part B—Putting it on its feet

Have students get up, stretch and walk around the room in character. Be very clear and do not allow students to make eye contact with each other. Tell students to imagine they are in the same space they pictured in their imagination. Have them walk around the drama room as if they were in that space. If it is a crowded space have them dodge others and if they are in a small space have them confine themselves to a corner in the room. Again allowing students the time needed to internalize each question, ask students the following:

1. Wouldn't you just love to tell someone exactly what is eating at you today?

2. Who could you tell?

3. Do you need to tell someone off? Or do you want to speak to someone who will really listen?

4. Do you owe someone an explanation?

5. Are you keeping something from someone?

6. Do you have something to vent about? What is it?

7. Imagine that person you need to speak with has just walked into your space.

8. How do you feel about them?

9. Are you excited to see them or do you want to dig a hole and disappear, run away or stay and speak?

10. Go over there and make your presence known to them.

Part C—Getting it all out

Tell students to freeze and look at you for further instruction. Inform them that they will be verbally addressing this other person momentarily on your "go" and they are not to pay any attention to anyone else in the room. This is not a performance but an exercise. Students should filter out the noise in the room and concentrate on what they need to do which is to address this individual they have selected to speak to.

If individual students look distracted, approach them discreetly and remind them that they need to focus on their own work and not be sidetracked by what others are doing. Simply saying "focus" kindly yet firmly usually does the trick. If several students in the class look distracted yell "Freeze!" to get everyone's attention and then repeat the instruction that no one should be looking at anyone else when they are working.

On your "go" have students approach their person B and rant for about a minute. Then yell "Freeze!" again. This time hand out pieces of loose-leaf and pens and say "Congratulations. You've just 'written' the first draft of your monologue." Have students write out what they just said to the best of their memory and collect papers. Even students who have little or nothing to say during the exercise will have their story in place by the time their pens hit paper. I've never seen a blank page yet!

Part D—Reading and listening

It's extremely important that you reassure students by explaining to them that not even Shakespeare himself had a winner on the first draft. A first draft is merely a place to begin to explore ideas and through a series of **staged readings** (reading on stage in front of the class) or **table reads** (reading for the director), students will have the opportunity to receive constructive feedback and refine their work into something that they are proud of.

A good place to start is by having students go up one by one to the stage area and read their monologues for the class. Invite students to give feedback to one another. Learning how to give articulate, creative and compassionate feedback to peers is an invaluable skill for your students to have. It's like having 20-some assistant directors! You do however have to be willing to share your director's chair with all of them when they get the hang of this! I wouldn't have it any other way. What a real tribute to your teaching to see students implement their skills and accomplishments by directing each other. It builds an ensemble atmosphere and without this team sharing component, teaching monologues would be a lonely and dry endeavour. For starters (students will learn more about directing in the **student directing exercises** to follow), teach them to point out good things and ask constructive questions like:

1. **Are the stakes high enough?** What happens if this character doesn't get what he needs from person B? What does he have to lose if he doesn't succeed? What is his definition of happiness?

2. **Should person B be someone else?** Perhaps the class has suggestions for an alternative person B. For instance if a waitress is telling the cook about her hot date last night and the monologue is comic, wouldn't it be even funnier if she were telling customers about it?

3. **Should the scene be set somewhere else?** For instance if the character is admitting to a crime, perhaps he should be at the police station rather than at a coffee shop.

4. **Why is he telling this secret to this particular individual?** While studying playwriting with Per Brask our class was taught to consider the following when analysing a character's behaviour: **You are a different person depending on who you are with.**

5. And more words of wisdom from Per: **What makes today different from any other day?**

Just as professional writers benefit from dramaturgical feedback and writers' circles, so do your students benefit from gaining constructive feedback from their peers. Teaching students to direct is one of the single most rewarding things a drama teacher can do. It engages students, allows them the opportunity to demonstrate concepts learned, gives them a feeling of ownership and it creates an ensemble atmosphere which is absolutely crucial in any drama classroom.

WRITING WHAT YOU KNOW

Let's face it. When we cast students for the big musical or theatrical production we expect them to play characters that are much older or younger than they are. It's just a fact of teaching drama that we will always be priming a white wig for some 14 year old to sport on stage whether we like it or not. Even for those of us who are moving away from finding students to fit scripts and towards creating scripts to fit students, we will always be attracted to directing a play or two that motivated us to pursue the theatre in the first place. We also mine up these classics because as drama educators we understand the vital importance of teaching students to be well versed in the theatre's most celebrated works of art.

But, there's a time and place for everything. When I first developed my unit on monologues, I did it to teach students how to strengthen their acting technique, direct, write and prepare for auditions. But most importantly I wanted to give students the opportunity to create their own gritty age-appropriate material. I wanted my students to tackle characters they knew something about, giving them the road map to act truthfully under imaginary circumstances. Wigs aside, I wanted my students to play real people and be moved by the sensation of truly understanding what **realism** means. I wanted them to be able to audition for parts with pieces that worked for them and I wanted them to be surrounded by ideas and issues that concerned young people, opening up a dialogue about what it's like to be a teenager today.

Here's how I did it. I repeated the **non-writing exercises**, this time insisting students select **teenagers** to observe. I also gave students these very simple rules to follow:

Your character must:

1. Be someone you could see a director casting you to play.

2. Be your age, sex and physical likeness.

3. Have a story worth telling.

4. Be based on someone you have personally come into contact with.

5. Be in a situation that has extremely high stakes.

The nice thing about getting students to create their own characters and stories is that they'll inevitably like the scripts they're working with; students who are interested in comedy will write comic pieces and students who are interested in dramatic pieces will write dramatically. Students will also write at the difficulty level they are comfortable with. It's a great exercise in differentiated instruction, which is a buzz word for teachers nowadays, given our vastly heterogeneous classes.

EDITING STUDENT WORK THE EASY WAY

Once students have gone through the **non-writing exercises** a couple of times, they should be ready to select a character that they are partial to and would like to work with for an extended period of time. After receiving some feedback from the group on their first draft, students will produce a second draft that will undergo your final approval.

Depending on your class, you may assign work for homework, or you may have students do all their work in class, collecting papers at the end of each session, insuring students have something to work from every time you meet. For those of us who've been around the block a couple of times, we'll know which classes work best under supervision and which classes need to take work home for further consideration.

As a former English teacher I still have nightmares of grading the never-ending paper trail. This will not be your experience here. It's really important that when you "edit" creative work in drama you don't use the opportunity to rewrite student work until it looks the way *you* think it should look. **Don't be a playwright!** Set up individual appointments with students, giving the rest of the class an activity to work on while you meet with students one by one to discuss and edit their work **together.**

You're not really "editing" written work, you're simply helping students get the work to a reasonable length and offering guidance on how to make the piece stronger. Think of it as teaching students to edit their own work. Sit back and give them feedback while they write notes and take a red pen to their own work. If you've ever judged public speaking, it's quite similar to the feedback you would give at the end of a speech or a debate. Your feedback relates to the presentation. You don't ask to see the student's piece of paper. What's on the paper is really insignificant at that point. You're looking at the presentation and giving feedback on how to make the verbal work out catchier.

Generally, your job will be to help students shorten. Listen for repeated sentences and ideas. That's usually the big one. The second most common mistake students make is having more than one story or using a great deal of exposition to describe a past event. Get rid of everything that isn't happening in the present, avoid repetition and make sure only one issue is being dealt with in the monologue and you should be able to assist students in editing their work to a reasonable length.

Ideally, student monologues should be no longer than 1 – 2 minutes. Directors in an audition situation would prefer to see two short polished pieces (one comic, one dramatic) from teens rather than one fairly lengthy piece that's under-rehearsed. Similarly, if you're planning on presenting your monologues as performance pieces, you don't want the audience to lose interest halfway through the show. You want the pieces to keep moving; the shorter the better. I still remember my grade 9 art teacher Mrs. Nickel telling us *"it's not quantity that's important, it's quality!"*

Here's a piece, of appropriate length, written by one of my students, Bruce (B.J.) Henry when he was in grade 11. B.J. performed this piece at the Manitoba Drama Youth Festival on Prairie Theatre Exchange's Mainstage in 2002. We wanted to bring pieces that had social significance to an audience filled with high school students from around the province. This piece scored high points with our young audience and you'll soon see why. Make note of the student's use of the word **beat** that he placed himself where he felt the character made a dramatic shift in his want or action and his keen understanding of **stakes, status** and **story structure.**

See Me

(Talking to the student body)

When you look at me, what is it that you see? Do you see a popular guy? Do you see a cute guy? Do you see a funny guy? Do you see a smart guy? *(beat)* Or do you see a gay guy? The reason why I ask is because for years I wondered that myself. I was carrying the weight of the world on my shoulders and I was scared to death to tell anyone who I really was. *(beat)* I was scared of what people would think. I was scared of what my parents would think and I didn't know how to tell them I was gay. I couldn't bear to see that painful look of disappointment on my dad's face when I would tell him I'm different from all the other sons on the soccer team. All these emotions and harsh feelings were being concealed until one day I had to do it. I decided to tell my parents and friends I was gay. I felt as if my hands were going to fall off from shaking so hard. My voice was weak and every fibre of my being wanted to back out at the very last second but I hung in there and told them. *(beat)* After it was over, all my fears seemed to slowly fade away. My parents didn't kick me out of the house and my friends didn't hate me. It was such a relief to finally be myself without leading a second life. There were no more games, no deceptions, no smoke and mirrors, *(beat)* just me, and it felt good, really good. As I look back on the experience I almost regret waiting as long as I did to come out of my closet. It would have been easier if I could have just said from the beginning "I'm gay!" but I couldn't because we live in a world full of labels and stereotypes. I wasn't the man society wanted me to be but I was the only man I could be.

Try to find material like this in a textbook for young actors. It's just not there. And there are so many other complex issues my students have tackled over the years including eating disorders, bullying, drug addiction, drunk driving, teen pregnancy and the list goes on and on. Give students the power to create their own dialogue and you'll be absolutely awestruck at what they come up with.

DIRECTING 101

So now that your students have a final draft of their monologue to work with, they need direction. And if you've done a solid job of teaching students the acting basics found in chapter 2, you can take this opportunity to sit back and watch your students display the skills they've learned by directing themselves and others. And what better way to engage your students than to empower them to teach each other.

I really can't see another way to teach a unit on monologues that does not involve student directing. It's the glue that ties the unit together and makes monologues interactive and ensemble oriented, something all drama lessons should be no matter what the content.

Student Directing Exercise #1—Table Reads

Pair students up; within each pair, have students decide who's the director and who's the actor. Each director will be given 20 minutes to conduct a **table read** (reading and analysing) of their partner's monologue. If you have a white board in the room, use it to list the following tasks the director should help the actor accomplish. Table reads should culminate in:

1. Clear actions and beats. What does the character want?

2. Ideas to make the **who, what, where** blatantly obvious.

3. Simple costume and prop ideas.

4. A clear understanding of the character's **stakes** and **status**.

When the 20 minutes are up have directors assume the role of actors and vice versa. Allow students the opportunity to have table reads with at least two different directors, accumulating as many ideas as possible to help them get started.

Some students choose to do some rewriting after their table reads and that's fine. Just make sure they show you what they've done so you're not surprised later.

Student Directing Exercise #2—Centres and Effort Actions

Pair students up with a new director. The director will help the actor experiment with different **centres** and **effort actions** by having the actor read her monologue while moving freely around the room. The director will make suggestions and point out what centres and effort actions appear to work and not work with the character. Again have students work for approximately 20 minutes in one role (director or actor) and then switch. Students should attempt this exercise with two or three different directors. When students feel they have articulated their characters' effort actions and centres they should use the time to refine those movements and make them clear in their monologue.

Directing Exercise #3—Establishing the Who, What, Where (Beginning) A.K.A The Janitor's Test

The importance of establishing the **who, what, where** in the first seconds of the scene was discussed in chapter 2.

Because students will only be using a mime box or chair for their set and minimal props and costumes—if an actor can't carry everything he needs for his monologue on one trip he has too many things—the onus is on the actor to make very clear in the first line of the monologue who they are, what they're doing and where they are.

This said, a perfectly selected costume piece (a volleyball jersey, for example), a simple prop (a textbook), an exemplification of status (a facial expression or hairstyle even) can give everything away even before an actor opens his mouth to let out a sound. The director should help the actor brainstorm ideas to make his who, what, where blatantly obvious as soon as the lights come up.

When ideas have been established, have actors bring in their costumes and props and try the beginning of their scene for a couple of directors and take away feedback to make the who, what, where even more clear to the audience.

My friend Cairn Moore calls it the **Janitor's Test.** She says if the janitor comes in to empty the trash and sees an actor for only seconds and knows exactly what the scene is about, the actor has passed the **Janitor's Test.** Have students do the Janitor's Test for the class using the first line of their monologue. Is the who, what, where clear? If not, the class can offer suggestions to help the actor make it more clear.

Student Directing Exercise #4—Stakes and Status (Middle)

This exercise will start out as a class exercise (Part A) and then develop into a pair actor/director exercise (Part B).

Part A

This is a repeating exercise. Using **centres** and **effort actions**, have students walk around the room in character. Ask students to select a powerful line in their piece. When they've decided on a line, have them repeat it out loud over and over again as they continue to walk around the room in character. Ask students to really listen to themselves say the line and internalize the implications of the line. An example would be B.J.'s line, "I'm gay." The actor really needs to hear himself say the line. Ask students: *What does it mean to say those words out loud? Who has the power in that line?*

Part B

In pairs, after discussing what was discovered in the repeating exercise, directors should help actors define their status on a scale ranking high, medium or low. Directors should help actors identify shifts in their character's status—if there are any—or identify the exact moment in the piece where the character loses or gains more power.

I've been lucky enough over the years to attend some really phenomenal acting workshops. I've remembered inspirational quotes from all of them and they have fuelled my teaching. Rick Skene taught me that power is handed on stage. **Actors are not in control of their own status.** The way others treat an actor on stage defines his status. When I heard this, a light-bulb went off in my head. The same principle applies to monologues. If an actor can articulate who they are to person B, then they can define their status.

Directing Exercise #5—Winning and Losing (End)

The Greeks called it the **anagnorisis.** It's the exact moment a character realises that he is the author of his own misfortune. There's no play if Oedipus does not have this moment. In general there is no play, comedy, tragedy or otherwise if the protagonist does not "get it." Having said this, when a character does arrive at his own epiphany, he also acknowledges, whether he's able to admit it or not, that he has either won or lost.

Pair students with a director again and have them help each other come up with three adjectives (follower, whiner, unmotivated) to describe their character. When students have come up with their adjectives, have them walk around the room in character repeating their three adjectives over and over again really internalizing their meaning. The words should affect their centres, effort actions, tone and inevitably give students that last piece of understanding they need to perform their monologue honestly and with unsurpassed understanding of the character.

GRADING

My only advice on grading is not to get into the trap of grading every little thing students do. Allow students the opportunity to learn and grow without the constant fear of being evaluated every time they attempt something in front of the class. There's no better way to get students nervous and set them up for failure than saying *"this is worth marks"* at the beginning of every exercise. Relax with the constant tallying of grades. Grade final presentations and assign an overall mark at the end of the unit that reflects students' participation in classroom exercises.

Consider allowing students to evaluate their own work on a grading rubric you've designed for the class. Later take the time to conference with each student individually discussing the appropriateness of the grade they have given themselves. If you haven't had students self-evaluate before, you'll be surprised to discover how hard they are on themselves; you'll be convincing them to grade higher!

This flexible and collaborative form of evaluation is more process oriented and respectful of students' individual journeys as artists.

The Anti-Writing, Editing and Directing Survival Kit

Writing

- **Never** tell students they will be writing.

- Create a space conducive to learning by de-cluttering your classroom.

- Teach students to base characters on real people they have personally come into contact with.

- Use the **non-writing exercises** to teach students about developing characters and stories.

- Allow students the opportunity to receive feedback from their peers through **table reads** and **staged readings**.

- Teach students to ask compelling questions during staged readings like: **what makes today different from any other day?**

- Students should base their characters on teenagers!

- Students' characters must:

  1. Be someone they can see a director casting them to play.

  2. Be their age, sex and physical likeness.

  3. Have a story worth telling.

  4. Be based on someone they have personally come into contact with.

  5. Be in a situation that has extremely high stakes.

Editing

- Don't be a playwright! Your job is to **help your students edit their own work.**

- Always edit *with* students.

- Help students bring their piece to an appropriate length and avoid repetition.

- Student written monologues should be no longer than 1-2 minutes.

Directing

- Empower students to teach each other!

- Table reads should culminate in:

    1. Clear **actions** and **beats**. What does the character want?

    2. Ideas to make the **who, what, where** blatantly obvious.

    3. Simple costume, prop and set ideas.

    4. A clear understanding of the character's **stakes** and **status**.

- Student directors should help actors:

    1. Experiment with **centres** and **effort actions**.

    2. Pass the **Janitor's Test**.

    3. Explore **stakes** and **status**.

    4. Articulate their character's **anagnorisis**.

Grading

- Don't grade everything.

- Consider letting students grade themselves on rubrics you've created.

Chapter 4: Your turn! Writing monologues for your students

If you hear a voice within you say "you cannot paint," then by all means paint, and that voice will be silenced.

—Vincent Van Gogh

So here's the truth about writing for students. It's rewarding, enlightening, humbling, frustrating and something you will never regret you did. Students love the prospect of their teacher writing for them. They get a kick out of it and you get an opportunity to try something new and test your creative juices for a captive audience. What writer wouldn't love to have eager actors ready to read their work and offer feedback day after day?

If you're apprehensive about writing because you've never done it before, you need not fear. The tools in this chapter will help you get those creative juices flowing and tap into your hidden potential. Have you ever wanted to write creatively but didn't know where to start? Have you ever thought you could write better teen material than what you've encountered on the market? Well here's your big chance. Give it a try and you'll be amazed at what you can do if you set your mind to it.

Use the monologues in chapter 5 for inspiration and to get ideas for themes. And when you see how short and to the point those monologues are, I assure you that you will feel much better about writing your own. This chapter will teach you easy tricks to get started in your new career as your high school's resident playwright. Your students will appreciate your efforts to cater to their interests and you'll be surprised how understanding and supportive they can be (especially if you've shown them the same courtesy in their work). So why not give it a try!

FINDING OUT WHAT THEY LIKE...SCARY!

As I mentioned in chapter 3, I am not particularly a fan of conventional writing exercises. Just like your students are not going to come up with ideas for writing sitting in a desk, you too will have no success staring at a computer screen trying to come up with innovative ideas for your students.

Think of yourself as your class's very own commissioned playwright. If you paid a playwright to come into your classroom (which I've done and I highly recommend you do if you ever have the opportunity and the funds to do so) you would expect him to meet with your students, get a feel for what they like and as a result come up with scripts that match your students' interests. Conversely, he would expect a supportive group of actors to work with that would afford him a **workshop** (students read work and offer feedback) period and time to do rewrites.

What I've done is made the above transaction concrete and easy for anyone to do by creating a worksheet (p.56 and 57) for students to fill out so that teachers can better understand what their students are looking for in a monologue. I use the information on the worksheet to instigate my own thought process. While I sometimes use little more than one suggestion on the entire worksheet, I do try to accommodate students' choice of **genre** (comic or dramatic) whenever I can. If I decide I want to see an actor perform a genre other than the one they've specified, or play a character unlike anything they've suggested to me on the worksheet, I'll consult with them first.

When you hand out your worksheet, encourage students to write any additional comments and suggestions in the space provided. However, some students prefer verbal requests. They'll track you down after class or the next day to give you a great idea for their character. Don't curb their enthusiasm. Hear them out and when they're finished, have them flip through your pile of worksheets and add their comments to their paper. You can't be expected to remember requests that are not written down on the worksheet.

As you'll notice in chapter 5, the monologues I write for students are quite short. I like short monologues for young people. They're easy to memorize, have the potential of becoming very polished and students are able to dust them off and relearn them on a moment's notice for audition purposes, festivals and school performances. It's also far less daunting for me to write short monologues for all my classes in a matter of weeks.

Acting Alone
Monologue Worksheet

Name:_____

Class: _____

Age: _____ Gender: _____

Your monologue will be based on some of the information that you give here.

All questions pertain to a hypothetical character and **not** you personally.

Economic status: (circle one)   High   Medium   Low

Personal status: (circle one)   High   Medium   Low

Interests: (make a list) (e.g.: sports, computer games, *Star Wars* movies, dating)

-
-
-

Fears: (make a list) (e.g.: dating, parents, teachers)

-
-
-

Accomplishments: (make a list) (e.g.: drama award, standing up to someone)

-
-
-

Possible Person B (someone your character is speaking to)
(e.g.: parent, friend)

-
-
-

Possible personal experiences your character is dealing with
(e.g.: drugs, unpopularity, detention)

-
-
-

Style: (circle one)   comic   dramatic

Comments/Suggestions: _____

_____

_____

_____

_____

_____

_____

_____

_____

_____

DEALING WITH REJECTION

OK, so you put yourself out there and give it your best shot and some of your students curl their eyebrows and start mumbling under their breath to their neighbour; what do you do? Relax. Remember the speech you gave your students when they wrote their own monologues? **No one should expect perfection from a first draft.**

What I like to do is hand out the monologues, giving students an opportunity to read their own piece a couple of times to themselves. I then ask students to write any questions or suggestions they may have right on the sheet that I've given them. Then I ask students to sit in a circle and read their monologues for the class. Students can give me their feedback at that time and I encourage feedback from the rest of the class as well. If I'm expected to make changes to the monologue, I take the monologue back from the student and all the suggestions and concerns that were vocalized to me should be recorded on that piece of paper. You shouldn't be expected to remember every little comment made by the class. **It's important that students give you their feedback in writing.**

Surprisingly, I haven't had to rewrite that many monologues. Working with students' suggestions, I've changed or added a couple of lines here and there but I remember having to start from scratch only a handful of times. Students are generally quite excited to have a piece written exclusively for them, and most, unless they're really unsatisfied, will work with what you've given them barring some minor changes.

Don't take it personally, however, if you have to rewrite. In the event that a student is really not pleased with their piece, sit down with them and ask them exactly what they want and go gracefully back to the drawing board. You'll find this is a rare occurrence and your edits will most likely be slight changes that you should be able to correct in no time at all. If you have your monologues on your computer with you, sometimes you can make the changes together with the students and print off a new copy right away.

KEEPING IT SHORT AND TO THE POINT

I have a few pointers to help you keep your process as short and sweet as possible. It shouldn't take you longer than a couple of evenings to write 20-30 monologues for one drama class. If you're planning on writing monologues for several classes you may want to disperse the workload throughout the term (a grade level a month for example) or semester to make the process more enjoyable and less stressful for you.

Regardless of how you want to divide the workload, here are some tips to make the process as manageable as possible:

1. **Keep a list of themes handy on your desk for inspiration.**
   Feel free to use themes more than once, in particular if you are writing for more than one class. Ideas for themes include:

   - Teen pregnancy
   - Abortion
   - Secrets
   - Drugs and alcohol
   - Sex and sexuality
   - Stealing
   - Bullying
   - Cheating
   - Dating
   - Breaking up
   - Moving
   - Partying
   - Divorce (parents)
   - Anorexia
   - Running away
   - Popularity

- Rejection

- Winning and losing

- Homework

- Sports

- School spirit

You can also ask your students to help you with a list of themes (write ideas on the board and later record them) or have the class decide on one theme for the entire class. The last set of monologues I wrote, half of the class played characters that were school bullies and the other half were victims of bullying.

2. **Always go with your first instinct.** When going through student worksheets take out a highlighter and only highlight the ideas that strike you as interesting the first time around.

3. **Write what you know!** As a teacher you encounter hundreds of teenagers every year. What better person to write about teens than someone who spends their entire day interacting with teens! Base your characters on students you have met along the way. You'll chuckle and have a great time mimicking their vocabulary, thoughts and general desires.

4. **Strike while the iron's hot.** Have students fill out worksheets in the afternoon and write the monologues that very night. Things students said that day and ideas that you wrote on the board will still be fresh in your mind.

5. **Observe and record.** When you notice students displaying interesting idiosyncrasies write it down. Record the way students speak to you or others. If you overhear something in the hallway that would make a great monologue idea, write it down as soon as you walk into your classroom. Think like a writer. Keep your eyes and ears open for interesting material—of which there is plenty in a high school!

6. And of course, don't forget to use some key points from chapter 3:

- Tell a story worth telling.

- What makes today different from any other day?

- What does the character want?

- What's at stake if the character doesn't succeed?

- Who has the power in the scene?

It's that easy! Enjoy the creative process and have fun!

The Teacher's
Writing Survival Kit

- Use the monologues in chapter 5 for inspiration.

- Think of yourself as your class's very own commissioned playwright.

- Have students fill out the **ACTING ALONE MONOLOGUE WORKSHEET.**

- Keep the monologues short and to the point.

- Relax. No one should expect perfection from a first draft.

- Have students give you their feedback in writing.

- If you have to rewrite, sit down with students and find out exactly what they want you to write.

- Remember these simple tips:

    1. Keep a list of themes handy for inspiration.

    2. Always go with your first instinct.

    3. Write what you know!

    4. Strike while the iron's hot.

    5. Observe and record.

- And of course, don't forget to use some key points from chapter 3:

    1. Tell a story worth telling.

    2. What makes today different from any other day?

    3. What does the character want?

    4. What's at stake if the character doesn't succeed?

    5. Who has the power in the scene?

Chapter 5: Or use mine!
100 scripted monologues for students

Art expresses human experience.

—Sanford Meisner in his book *Sanford Meisner on Acting*

It's good to have a selection of monologues on hand to use for classroom acting exercises, audition purposes (to create MONO-LOGUE CHEAT SHEETS, chapter 6), scene analysis and even for public performances. Perhaps you are pressed for time and would like to teach students to perform monologues but don't want to get into the writing and editing process. Or perhaps you are introducing monologues for the first time in your classroom and would like students to read and analyze some already scripted monologues for starters.

Whatever your reasons for wanting to use scripted monologues in lieu of creating original pieces, here is a selection of monologues I've written for students over the years that I believe you will find useful. All of the monologues in this chapter were written with specific students in mind, underwent a workshop whereby students made suggestions for improvements and have been used as classroom exercises, audition pieces or performance pieces. While monologues are categorized by gender and genre, you'll notice that some monologues overlap genres and can even, in places, be performed by students of either gender.

Some are longer, shorter, easier, more difficult, but they're all fun to do and most importantly student approved!

Comic Monologues for Young Women

Sleeplessness

(speaking to a friend)

It feels like I haven't slept in weeks. Maybe because I probably haven't slept in weeks. I can't keep my eyes open. Who's that over there? It looks like Tony Bruns. Did you know that Tony Bruns used to date Sara Louis who lives in 602 but while he was dating her he was also dating Margie Porter who lives in 306? Now he's coming out of 403? Who lives in 403? Oh my god. There's Mr. Fender getting out of Mrs. Lander's room like 12 minutes before Mr. Lander gets home. They're like 28 minutes later than usual. And there's Sissy Mayor walking Mr. Sander's dog again. She only walks his dog because she's hoping he'll die and give her his life savings. What a terrible thing to do. And there's Fanny Chandler talking to Mr. Lander. I hope she's not telling him that his wife is having an affair with Mr. Fender. I wish people would just mind their own business.

A Mistake

(speaking to her teacher)

F?!? I think there's been some mistake here. Mr. Smith, are you sure this F doesn't belong on someone else's paper? Your hand could have maybe slipped. It was supposed to hit Jamie's paper and instead ended up on mine. I mean, I've never gotten an F. I've never seen my name and an F on the same paper. I'm an A+ student, and sometimes teachers take the liberty of putting an extra + on the page making it an A++ paper. Like today I've received an A+ in math an A++ in science and an A+ and a thank you card from my English teacher. So this is surely a mistake. I'm sure it happens. But when you correct it, could you please white out the F completely. I can't bear to look at it.

Fitting in

(speaking to a friend)

Maybe if I smoked, I could hang out with Tiffany's group. Like they're out there all the time smoking and chatting. Chatting and smoking. I could smoke. How hard could it be? But I don't know what brand they all smoke. I have to get closer so I can see. It's a grey pack. What do you know about cigarettes? Any idea what kind the grey pack is? Oh my god. I'm a complete loser.

It's Over

(speaking to a boyfriend)

You're dumping me? You can't dump me. We just started dating. Everyone thinks we're dating. You're a real jerk you know that. I did it with you. Do you think I would have done it with you if I knew you were gonna dump me right away? That's like an unspoken rule. We have to go out for another three weeks at least. And if we don't, I'm gonna tell everyone things about you that you don't want told. Ha! Dumping me? And after three weeks, I dump you, in public in front of everyone. Who do you think you are? Dumping me? No one dumps me. I'm dumping you!

The Confession

(speaking to a priest)

Forgive me father for I have sinned. It's been 4 months since my last confession… Well I guess my confession is that I really don't have a confession. I signed up to get out of a math test. Sister Mary said that our spiritual well-being is more important than Mrs. Quaker's morning math quiz. I tend to agree because I didn't study for the quiz. I was out last night with my friends. We went to a rave. That's confession worthy, isn't it? There were drugs there. I didn't take any. I had a sip of vodka and then I spit it out. There was no mix. I danced with a boy from St. Vincent. He was really cute. He's too old for me. I bet that's confession worthy! He didn't touch me inappropriately or anything like that. You're not gonna call St. Vincent's, are you? I'd hate to get him in trouble. I'm still expecting a call from him. I'll go back to class now.

The Talk

(speaking to her mom)

Mom, I want you to give me the "talk." You know the one with the birds and the bees that everyone seems to have gotten except for me. I feel the need to hear it. From you. So if you could make it entertaining and enlightening at the same time, I'd really appreciate it. I took the liberty of downloading some diagrams off the Internet. I'm hoping that they'll help in your presentation. My teacher says I'm a visual learner... I know I'm 16, but we haven't done this and I feel that it's necessary. Everyone seems to know where everything goes and how and why except me. You dismissed me from Family Life and now I'm in the dark, like the people were in the dark before Prometheus gave them light. I want to be enlightened and feel like I can have a frivolous conversation with my peers in the girls' change room. OK, I'm ready. Take your time. I've been waiting for this for a long time. Popcorn?

The Detention

(speaking to another student)

All right. This detention thing sucks. I put in my hour. Why am I still sitting here? You know, we have to stop doing this. I'm not taking the blame for other people's stupid actions anymore. I'm tired of it. Let them serve their own stupid detentions. I bet Karen and her friends are at home right now, plotting another detention for us tomorrow. I think it's time to get them into trouble. *(beat)* I have a great idea.

The Ex

(speaking to an ex-boyfriend)

Since we're not going out anymore, Fredrick, I just want to lay out some ground rules. You are not to say hi to me in any capacity, not in the hallways, not at a game and not at a party held by a mutual friend. When I say hi to you, you know it means I hate you but I'm being polite because someone who I'm trying to impress is in the near vicinity. When you find someone else to go out with, which may very well be in the distant future, you are to tell her that I was a superior girlfriend and she has big shoes to fill even though I don't have a jealous bone in my body and I could care less who you date. I prefer that you inform me through e-mail if you've met someone so I can prepare nice things to say about our now fizzled but at one time loving relationship. Now please get out of my face.

The Driving Lesson

(speaking to the examiner)

Look, the pillars were not people, they were pillars. If they were people and I truly killed someone then I agree with you that I do not deserve to pass the test. But since I didn't kill anyone, I think hitting one pillar out of 4 is pretty good odds that I'll drive home without killing a real person along the way. *(beat)* I don't think you understand my situation, Bob. Today is my 16th birthday. Every 16-year-old gets his or her license on the day of his or her special-legal-to-drive-to-the-mall birthday. If I don't show up at my friend Natalie's party tonight driving the teal CRV that my parents bought for me I'm going to be the laughingstock of my grade. *(beat)* Can I try it again? I promise I won't hit the pillar this time, Bob.

The Sibling

(speaking to her little sister)

Look. You can't come in here whenever you feel like it. You take my things, don't put them back, leave a mess and never clean it up. I'm sick of it. You can't borrow my things anymore, and you can't come in here anymore. I'm changing the lock. The only time you can come in here is if you are bringing me something, like a present: money, food, my things that you've taken! Otherwise stay out. Live in your own room. Stay away from me and my things. Got it? *(beat)* Can I borrow your boots tonight?

Not My Type

(speaking to her boyfriend)

It's not you it's me…No it's you. You're just not my type. You're kinda boring. If there was a nicer word, I'd use it, but there isn't. Boring's the right word. And you're kinda insecure for a guy. I've watched you comb your hair in the mirror and ruin it and fix it and ruin it and fix it…girls do that. I just don't want to date a girl. There's nothing wrong with dating girls, but if I wanted to date a girl, I'd date a girl. I'm looking for a boyfriend. Someone who tells interesting guy stories and has guy hair and hangs out with other guy guys. Someone who smells like football and is rude at the dinner table and forgets to call me back and slams the door in my face. I like that. I'm sorry. You're just not for me.

Aliens

(speaking to her teacher)

Mrs. Peters, I'm not going to tell you the aliens abducted my homework again. I know you're growing tired of that excuse. My homework is being analyzed by aliens. I will get it back and you will get it tomorrow. OK, now that that's settled, I thought I'd swing my science fair idea by you. I'm currently creating a brain trap for the aliens who frequently visit me at night. The idea is to allow them to think they are entering my bedroom unnoticed and then when they least expect it my brain trap, which is a computerized remote control operated hockey helmet, will drop on one of their heads and they'll be trapped because the helmet will be attached to a chain that is attached to my ceiling fan and then...should I do my homework here or in study hall?

The Sale

(speaking to a friend)

You missed the sale. I don't know what you were doing that could have been more important, but you missed it. Gone. It's gone. The sale. No more clothes. No more sale. I hope your plans were more important than me. Me and the sale. It would almost be OK if there was something more important than the sale, but me? What was more important than shopping at a sale with me? I bought four pairs of shoes and you can't wear them... except maybe if you let me borrow your eyelash sweater. Then maybe you can borrow my shoes, that I bought on sale...alone.

Call Me

(speaking to a friend)

OK this is just between you and me. I did something just wild yesterday. I called him. Johnny. I know I said I would never have the guts to do it but I psyched myself up and I did it. It was fantastic. It really was. I got on the phone and called him. I didn't talk to him of course; that would be way too ridiculous. I just waited for him to say hello and then I hung up…around fifteen times. Oh my God I hope he doesn't have call display.

The Essay

(speaking to her teacher)

No no no no no no no. I can't fail this term, Miss Toby. If I fail my parents will ground me and I won't be able to go to the dance. And dances are for kids like me who like to hang out with their friends and meet cute boys and dance the night away. I will really honestly do anything to get out of missing the dance. *(beat)* I can write another essay tonight and it'll be the best English essay you've ever seen, I swear. It'll be most improved student material and you'll love it. And let's not even mention how rewarding it will be for you, the teacher, to see such a turnaround in your student. How 'bout I get that essay to you first thing tomorrow morning?

Philanthropy 101

(speaking to her friend)

I cannot believe that he said all those things about me. Like as if I'm egotistical and vain. I'm the furthest thing from being vain. I always let old people have my seat on the bus and I give to charities that put their little plastic cups out at the coffee shop. What more am I expected to do?!? Did he want me to volunteer at a homeless shelter? Would that have made me less "egotistical?" How dare he label me like that. He doesn't know me. He thinks he knows me but really he doesn't. I can be a very caring and generous person. What does he know anyway?

Ugly on the Inside

(speaking to a friend in the bathroom)

Do you think I look fat in these jeans? Oh forget it. Don't even bother lying to me. I'm horrible. I'm fat. I'm even fatter than Jane and she's huge. She has a bigger bum than me but she's gross. I mean disgusting. I *cannot* be compared to that hideous skank in any way. I have to lose 10 pounds. If I don't, people will talk. Do you think people are already talking about me? Oh my God. Of course people are talking about me. We talk about everyone who has something wrong with them behind their backs why wouldn't they talk about me? What do I do? I can't go to class with fat thighs. People will laugh at me. That's my job! That's what I do. I laugh at people because there's something wrong with them. I can't have people laughing at me. That's not how things work. *(gathering her things)* I'm just gonna go home and come back when I've lost 10 pounds. Tell my teachers I'm sick or something. Oh my God. Oh my God. *(quickly makes an exit)*

The Geek

(speaking to a friend)

(dressed as a typical "geek" and sitting in front of a pile of books) Who does she think she is anyway—Jennifer Aniston? I mean give me a break. She walks around this school like she's the cat's meow. Everyone knows she's had a nose job. Remember the nose she had in elementary school? Oh God. I can't believe people don't hold that against her. Everyone like worships her. She's such a bitch. I hate her. I wish…I wish…she moves and has to go to another school where everyone is better looking than her and people tease her and laugh at her in her gym shorts. She deserves that. Oh, even better, I hope Ric dumps her. *(beat)* That would be divine retribution. *(looks at her watch)* Oh I gotta finish her homework before she gets here or she'll be real mad. I don't want that. *(starts scribbling frantically)*

Pre-cal

(speaking to a teacher)

(holding on to pre-cal test) I passed? How is that possible? This is the first calculus test I've ever passed. I'm gonna cry. *(beat)* There must be some sort of error. *(takes out calculator to verify error)* This can't be true. I'm speechless. I'm absolutely speechless. *(beat)* I passed! *(dancing around)* I passed calculus or pre-calculus. Whatever. It's all the same. I'm a genius! I rule! I get it! I get calculus! *(beat)* I can tutor. How cool is that? Students can pay me for my "knowledge." Right on. Where can I sign up?

The Frog

(speaking to a teacher)

(wearing a lab coat and holding a scalpel) I'm sorry, I don't dissect things. I signed up for this class because I was told there was no math. No one mentioned we'd be cutting up frogs. I'm against cutting up frogs or anything that has *(looks down at the table and then up again)* legs. I really don't know what you want to do about this but I'm firm on this point. I won't be dismembering little green things that used to hop on lily pads saying "ribit." Sorry for the inconvenience. *(handing over the scalpel)* I won't be needing this.

COMIC MONOLOGUES FOR YOUNG MEN

The Goldfish

(speaking to his little brother, holding a fish bowl with a baby carrot floating on top)

Look Michael…*(beat)* he's sleeping. But because we love him so much and want him to be with his family, we're gonna flush him down the toilet. OK Michael? The toilet water is going to flush out into the beautiful pond where Fluffy's family lives, OK? *(goes to flush, stops)* Michael. Stop crying. I just finished telling you that the stupid fish is alive and going to swim with his mommy in a beautiful pond so why are you still crying? Stop that. *(looking at his little sister)* Melissa, tell him to stop crying. Oh why are you crying?!? No we can't flush your one-eyed rabbit down the toilet too. He's too big, Four Eyes! Look kids, the 25-cent goldfish is dead and I'm flushing him down the toilet so some nice sewer rat can eat him for lunch. And despite what Nana Louise tells you there is no afterlife. When you die some fat guy is gonna to throw a pile of dirt on you and call it a day. So go eat your salami sandwiches and when you're done I'll take you to Fish Land and get you another fish. *(to little sister)* Don't look at me. Mom's only paying me $5 an hour. I can't afford to buy you another stuffed animal. *(beat)* He's not dead yet.

The Workout

(speaking to himself)

OK, I'm ready for my workout. *(flexing arms)* I look hot. I am hot. No I'm not. I will be hot. Yeah. That's good. I'm gonna get in shape. I'm gonna be the man! Oh who am I kidding? This working out thing is not gonna work. No one's gonna look at me. *(beat)* Hey, maybe if I had a special talent…like if I could stand on my head or do a cartwheel. Maybe then I'd be cool. Or maybe not. Push-ups. I'll start with push-ups. *(he gets down on the floor to do push-ups)* And one.

Good News

(speaking to his parents)

Mom, Dad, I want to be a priest. I want to devote my life to God. And I'm serious about this, so I don't want you to try to talk me out of it. I'm not asking your permission either; I'm telling you that this is what I think I'm meant to do. *(beat)* It's good news! You can smile or laugh or congratulate me or any of those things. I love God…and I love you. I really need you to give me some response, any response.

Stealing the Exam

(speaking to his teacher)

Yes I did it. I stole the exam. And I'm not going to say that I'm sorry. I want to be punished. Publicly if possible. Stealing that exam is the best thing that ever happened to me. Students talk to me. Some even know my name. I went from geek boy to popular, very popular, overnight. I'm not going to apologize to anyone. In fact you need to be apologizing to the principal for having your exam in an accessible location. You're the one who looks silly here. I look great. I hope I get in big shit for this.

Making the Gang

(speaking to a gang member, wearing "gang" attire)

OK, so don't get me wrong, I want to be a part of your gang. I'll do all the things you told me to do except steal from Mr. Chan. I won't do that. He gave me my first job, and I don't have anything against him. I'll steal from someone else. Someone I don't know. *(beat)* How about I steal the newspapers from the corner of the street in the morning? That would really inconvenience the neighbourhood. Think about it.

Trying to study

(speaking to a neighbour through a closed door)

Sir. I don't want to be rude or anything but I was wondering if you could turn your music down. I love opera. I really do, but I'm studying for a math exam and the walls in this apartment building are paper thin. If I could drive, I'd go to the library to study, but I don't drive, and I'm babysitting my little sister right now…I said I have a math exam and I'm babysitting my sister…my sister. Sir, you really need to turn the music down if you want to hear what I'm saying…I said could you please turn down the music… Turn down the music please… Turn down the music… SHUT THE MUSIC YOU OLD FART I'M TRYING TO STUDY FOR A STINKING EXAM AND BABYSIT MY LITTLE SISTER YOU FREAK!… Thank you. Have a nice night.

The Apology

(speaking to his parents)

I know I wasn't supposed to throw a party and I went behind your back and that was obviously bad. But there was no harm done right? So the pool has a little bit of a vodka taste to it. It's clear. No one will know but us. And I've sent the rug that Matthew got sick on to the dry cleaners. Marcy knows this great guy that gets cigarette burns out of carpet like it's no one's business. I could have him here by the afternoon. I found this chandelier at Value Village that looks pretty much like Grandma's. I don't even think she'll notice that it's missing. Look. I'm really sorry. Maybe next time you go to Hawaii you should take me with you. I'm not as responsible as you make me out to be.

Money Problems

(speaking to his dad)

Dad, I have a problem. I was at the music store, and my credit card didn't work. The cash register lady said I was over my limit. So then I went to the bank machine and put my Interac card in and the machine ate it. Then I walked to the parking lot, and my car was being repossessed... Is there something I don't know about here? Like we do still have money, right? Lots and lots of money? I mean I'm still the richest and therefore coolest kid in school right? *(looking around)* It's OK, Dad. I've had a rough week. I'm sure I'm dreaming this. My imagination is probably just getting the best of me. I'm still rich. Richie Richard. Richie Ric. Yeah. Maybe if I just go to my room and put my head down and take a nap this will all be sorted out. OK, sorry to bother you, Dad. I know you're busy working, making money so I can spend it and be cool. I'm cool. I'm still cool. It's all cool. See you later Dad, standing in front of your Mercedes holding a cell phone and not crouched over your desk holding your head. Catch you later, Dad.

It Wasn't Me

(speaking to his dad)

I wasn't speeding, OK. I don't know what old lady McFearson thinks she saw, but it wasn't me speeding. Lots of kids have the same car as me. I'm not taking the blame for this. Someone else, driving a car like mine, scared old lady McFearson out of her crazy mind last night, but it wasn't me. Jeez. I'm sick of her and her stupid accusations. Last week I ran over her garbage cans. Last summer I stole her Christmas lights. She's nuts, Dad. She thinks everyone's out to get her. Well I've had it. I'm finally gonna take a stand. I'm gonna go over there right now and tell her that she needs to get glasses and leave me out of her crazy hallucinations...Can I at least call my friends and tell them that I'm grounded?

The Audition Piece

(speaking to an audition panel)

Hi. My name is Sandy Sullivan and I'll be performing a monologue from *Romeo & Juliet*. I will play the part of Romeo. *(looks at his piece of paper, looks at the panel)* I seem to have brought the wrong piece of paper. I brought my shopping list. I can perform my shopping list instead if you don't mind. *(clears his throat and tries to make it as romantic and dramatic as his Romeo monologue could have been)* Toothpaste. *(looks at paper)* Mouthwash. Toilet paper. Orange juice with calcium. Beef jerky. Thank you for your time.

The Feared Floor

(speaking to a hotel clerk)

Ah sir...I noticed that my hotel room is on the 14th floor. Who are we kidding, sir? The 14th floor is really the 13th floor. The unlucky floor. The feared floor. I was just wondering if maybe you could move me to another floor. One with less doom associated with it. So if you could just look for a happier floor on your computer there that would be fantastic, sir. I know you're really busy and I'm really very happy to wait as long as it'll take you to find me a more inviting floor. And another thing, when you've done that, could you please have someone escort me through the building and show me the proper escape route in case of a fire? And if there's an alternate escape route due to another form of emergency, could you have my escort show me that as well? I'm on a school trip and my parents are expecting me home in three days and I intend to get home safely. So if you could take care of that, sir, that would be greatly appreciated. A better floor and a tour of the escape routes. Thanks a bunch.

Misunderstood

(to a guidance counsellor)

No one understands me. I guess I like it that way. Elvis was misunderstood. Shag carpeting is often misunderstood. Sock puppets, nobody appreciates the art of sock puppetry anymore.

Leprechauns, another misunderstood phenomenon. They only want some respect...I would describe myself as a '67 Mustang convertible *(mimes driving)* on the road of life, wind blowing through my hair and going nowhere in particular and really not caring I don't know where I'm going. I think people generally like me. I think the chicks dig me. I think I got the right moves. I wish I had a Mustang. *(looks at his watch)* So how much longer do I have to talk to you anyway?

Kitchen Duty

(speaking to a teacher, Mr. Richards)

Look Mr. Richards, I know I shouldn't have put gum on your chair...but it was funny. Everyone said it was funny. *(beat)* I can't get a detention. My mom says if I get one more detention I'm gonna have to switch to kitchen duty. Do you know what kitchen duty is, Mr. Richards? I have five siblings, two parents, one grandmother and a dog. Kitchen duty is what they make you do in hell. I have to wash all the dishes after every meal, sweep the floor and mop. But it's not really mopping. Mopping is what normal people do. My mom insists on cleaning the floor with a sponge! Who does that? I can't be on kitchen duty.

Dance Class

(speaking to the dance teacher)

Hi. I heard about your dance class on the announcements and I think I want to sign up. But I'm not gay. I like to dance, break dance mostly, sometimes rap. I don't want to wear any tights or any shit like that. I just wanna dance, like funky stuff. I heard you do that kind of thing. But I really don't want to wear any tights. I won't wear any tights. I'll tie my hair back and that's about it. So I heard there's no other guys in this class and I'm OK with that. Because I'm not gay. I'm here for the girls. All the hot sweaty girls and to learn some better moves. As long as that's clear we're cool. Cool. Where do I get changed?

Impressing Lindsey

(speaking to a friend)

Hey, check out this new move. *(shows move on his skateboard, it's horrible)* Do you think it'll get me to the Olympics? I'm trying to get on the team to impress Lindsey. She said, "Tod, if you make the Olympics, that would be real cool." Can you believe that? Can you believe how much she likes me? I'd love to sit and chat, but I have to perfect this move if I'm gonna go to the Olympics and score a date with Lindsey. "Real Cool."

The Crush

(looking up from a book and speaking to a friend)

You know that spider's been living in that corner for about a month. I think it probably has kids and satellite by now. Hey Mark, can I ask you a question? Do you think Sarah will go out with me if I enter the pie-eating competition? I'm thinking she'll probably think I'm cool if she sees me scarf down an entire pie in 43 seconds. That was my record last year…The reason I'm asking you is, well I don't really know what she likes, other than school. Like I don't really know anything about her and I want to break the ice somehow and have a basis for a conversation. Do you think the pie will help? *(beat)* Oh my God. She's looking at me. Do I look OK? Should I smile at her? She's not smiling at me. OK, now she's smiling at me. I'm gonna smile back. *(awkward smile)* Bad idea. I think she's talking about me. I want to die. *(covers his face with his book)*

The Haircut

(looking in the mirror, talking to a friend)

You don't like my haircut? My mom cut it. She cuts all of our hair. She bought a book, *How to Cut your Family's Hair,* and now she thinks she can. You know, this isn't as bad as *Cooking Organically* or *How to Talk to your Teen* or our all-time favourite, *Family time without the TV.* In fact, she can keep cutting our hair if it means no more "How to" books. I don't mind my hair at all. And if anyone says anything about it, I'll kick the crap out of them.

Hey Bus Driver

(speaking to the bus driver)

Hey… Hey, Mr. Bus Driver. Do you think you could *(mocking singing)* speed up a little bit, speed up a little bit…*(to another passenger)* Shut up. I paid my fare. This sucks. *(to the bus driver)* You suck. Your whole stupid public establishment sucks…the big one. When you woke up in the morning, I bet you looked forward to driving this bus. I'm sure you felt ready to start your stupid, pathetic day driving the public around town, again and again. Well I got somewhere to be, Mr. Bus Driver. You're cramping my style. *(combs his hair)* Look, if I don't get to the arena in five minutes flat, people that are waiting for me won't be people that are waiting for me anymore. They'll be people who aren't waiting for me anymore. Have a heart, man. Just press the pedal a little. *(looking at his watch)* I have an image to uphold here, pal. *(beat)* Hey mister, I'm sorry I made fun of your job. I know you probably have a family to feed and such, but I got a girl waiting for me. You must remember what that was like… How 'bout you skip a couple of stops and do a kid a favour. You'd be in my good books. I'll send you business. *(waits, big smile)* Thanks, man.

The Rejection

(speaking to a girl)

(whispering and looking over his shoulders to make sure no one's looking) What do you mean you don't want to go out with me? But I'm captain of the hockey team. I'm the cutest boy in the class. I'm smart, funny, polite…this has never happened to me. I'm having a feeling I've never experienced before. *(beat)* Oh my God, it's embarrassment. I'm embarrassed. You've embarrassed me. Oh please, please don't tell anyone you turned me down. That would be the end for me. I would never live that down. Boys are so cruel.

The Big Date

(speaking to a friend)

(counting money) So do you think seventeen dollars is enough to take Stephanie out on a date? It's probably enough; it's just that it looks stupid you know not having a twenty. It looks like I scrounged up the money from family and friends – which is what I *did* – but it just looks bad. Oh well, one day when I'm a doctor and I'm rolling in it we'll look back on this, her and I, and we'll laugh. *(beat)* I just hope she doesn't laugh at me tonight.

The Come On

(speaking to a girl)

Wanna come over to my house to play video games? It'll be cool; I have lots of games for my Playstation and my dad just bought this massive plasma TV to play them on. It's wicked. You'd really like it. I'll even give you a head start, that way it'll be fair. I'm all about being fair. *(beat)* You're cute. Wanna kiss?

A Friendly Misunderstanding

(speaking to a classmate)

No I don't want to fight you! You can have the girl, dude. I didn't know she was your girlfriend. If I knew I wouldn't have gone anywhere near her. Trust me! Why would I be so stupid with you being so big and me being so small? I'd have to be an idiot and do I look like an idiot? I'm on the honour roll. Surely I'm not an idiot. Well now that we seem to have cleared up this misunderstanding, I'll be heading back to class where I will certainly not say a word to Susan who is now clearly known to be your girlfriend. I'll even do you a favour and save you some future difficulty by spreading the word.

The Man

(speaking to another student holding a sandwich)

I can say whatever I want to whoever I want. Who the hell are you? You must be new to not know who I am. Let me introduce myself. I'm Dan the man. I own this school and everyone in it.

You got that, punk? Everyone in this building does what I want when I want. When I snap my fingers like this *(snaps like the Fonz)* everyone in this place comes running. *(mimicking)* "Oh what do you need, Dan?" "What can I get for you, Dan?" "Were your fries not hot enough, Dan?" That's right. I say jump and everyone says how high. Even the teachers are afraid of me. *(pulls out report card)* Straight A's and I can't even read. So now that you're enlightened on how things work around here, why don't you just go on your merry little way and we'll pretend this day never happened. But when I see you here tomorrow I'll expect to see you singing an entirely different tune. *(takes a bite of the sandwich)* And tell your mom to put some mayonnaise in your sandwich next time. And maybe a bag of chips.

The Attack

(speaking to a group of students)

Just one thing before you beat me up; please don't hit me in the face because I have to work tonight and because my mom will get upset and she'll call the school and I'll have to tell on you and then we'll be here all over again. OK. Go. *(closing his eyes tight and then opening them suddenly)* Just one more thing. I appreciate the fact that I have to be beaten up; I did rat on you guys but do you really think it's gonna take more than one of you to do a satisfactory job? I mean history will tell you that I don't fight back and it's probably more effective for you guys to use only one goon considering it will conserve energy that you can use to beat up other defenseless students who didn't go looking for a fight in the first place. OK. On your own time. *(closes eyes and then opens them again)* And just to make something clear here, I might have told on you guys but weren't you really better off returning Mrs. Fletcher's car and admitting your wrongdoings to the police? And your debt to society will only be a few months max. *(beat)* Thanks for your time. I know you're very busy stealing cars and whatnot. I'm ready. *(closes eyes tightly)*

DRAMATIC MONOLOGUES FOR YOUNG WOMEN

No favours

(speaking to a co-worker)

No, I'm not covering for you. Forget it. You're on your own. *(looks around before speaking)* If you want to steal merchandise then go right ahead. I'm not your mother; I'm not gonna to stop you but I'm certainly not going to help you either. I took this job because I wanted to make a little extra money, not because I wanted to end up with a criminal record or worse in the slammer. Take your chances but don't say I didn't warn you.

The Decision

(speaking to a doctor)

I read your pamphlet and I still would like to do this. I'm 18, so I don't need permission from a parent. I'd like to have an abortion. I'm not ready to be someone's mother. I'm not even really ready to be an adult, whatever that is. I made a mistake. I'd like to have a baby one day, but with someone else and when I'm ready. I'm not ready right now.

Shopping

(speaking to a store clerk)

I think you should stop staring at me. I'm not gonna to steal anything. I have money in my wallet. I do have a job, and drive a car. I have a phone too. Why would I steal anything from your store? You don't have to pretend you're not following me. I know you don't trust me, OK, I'm not stupid. It's nothing new. I get stared at a lot by people who look just like you. I don't think I want to buy anything from your store. I do think I'd like to write a letter to your manager *(reading the nametag),* Sara. I'll let him or her know how you stole business from this company. Stare at someone who looks like a criminal next time.

Once Upon a Druggie

(speaking to a probation officer)

Look I don't do drugs anymore. This is a big mistake. I didn't sell or give any drugs to any little kids, OK. I'm off. I haven't even seen any drugs in two months, so you have the wrong girl. You know this is typical. I clean up and this is what happens. What's the point in cleaning up? Everyone still looks at you like you're a druggie. "Oh look, there's Tina's daughter. Like mother like daughter; isn't that a shame. The sins of the mother don't go unnoticed to her children. Poor girl. She'll never amount to anything. They should have taken her away while there was still a chance." *(beat)* I have a job now. I've been in school every day for an entire month. Just call the school and ask. I'm doing exactly what you told me to do. But it doesn't make a difference because I'm still here, aren't I?

The Fix

(speaking to a student)

Jake, you think maybe I could have some more of that stuff you gave me last week? The stuff you got from your little brother. The *(spelling it out)* R-I-T-A-L-I-N. *(beat)* Don't look at me like you don't know what I'm talking about. You can't give me that shit and then take it away. I need it now. I was on fire this week. I did all my work, got an A on my calculus test, had time to play volleyball, go to rehearsal, work and make a ton of tips. Where are my drugs? Listen you little twit. The only reason I even spoke to you was because you told me you could help me. So I want more. I don't care what you have to do. Don't come to school tomorrow unless you have something for me. Got it?

Parents

(speaking to her mother)

Look, I don't drink a lot, just a little bit of vodka before bed. Usually when you and Dad are busy yelling at each other. That's when I do it. That's when I wish I was someone else, living somewhere else in a quiet house and not here with you. I drink because I hate being in this house. I hate falling asleep in my bed listening to the two of you treat each other like animals. I'm sorry you're unhappy. I'm sorry you gave up your dreams to marry Dad and have me. I'm really really sorry. But I drink myself to sleep. And I'm not sorry about that. You need to be sorry about that.

The New Neighbour

(speaking to a new neighbour)

(extremely shy) I couldn't help but notice that you just moved in. I saw you in your driveway yesterday and thought I should come over and introduce myself. I'm Tammy. I live next door on this side. I got really excited when I heard that someone my age was moving in. I don't have anyone to hang around with in the summer. There aren't a lot of kids on this street. *(beat)* I'm an only child too. It would be nice to have someone to talk to instead of my parents every now and then. Well I won't keep you. Come over any time.

Good Bully

(speaking to a bully)

Hey! Hey! What the hell do you think you're doing? Give her back her book. How old are you? Do you think it's cool to pick on someone just because she's smaller than you? Get a life. Take your loser friends and get outta here. School's over. What are you hanging around here for? I'm assuming you're not waiting for a ride. So scram or I'll give you a new appreciation for literature when I take my own personal copy of *Of Mice and Men* and hit you over the head with it.

The Move

(speaking to a school counsellor)

I guess it wouldn't be so bad if I hadn't made a friend. Last year we moved three times and that was fine because I never had enough time to make a friend. Usually that's how it works. We don't stay in one spot long enough for me to make a friend; so moving becomes more inconvenient than anything else. I was smart last time; I didn't even unpack my boxes. But this time, I unpacked and I made a friend.

Cheater

(speaking to her boyfriend)

I can't believe you cheated on me. *(beat)* I'm not even mad. I just can't believe it. I thought this was going really well and then I heard what you did and...I just don't understand. Why? There has to be a reason why you would do this to me. I feel like such an idiot.

Oh Captain

(speaking to a friend)

If we lose another game, I'm gonna hurt someone. I can't be the cheerleader for a losing team that sucks as bad as ours does. I'm sick of telling everyone that we're gonna win the next one, when we're not! How could we? And everyone's looking at me like I have the answers or something. I don't. I hate being the one that everyone blames or looks at for some sort of reassurance. I quit. I can't be captain when I don't even believe in the team.

This Feeling

(speaking to a boyfriend who's sleeping)

I feel something weird and I don't know what it is. It could be love, but it could be something else. I guess I don't really know what love is but I feel something and I'm willing to call it love if you're willing to tell me you feel something too. I love you. I really love you. *(beat)* I'm scared that I'm the only one here having this feeling.

Quitting

(speaking to a parent)

I can't keep up with it anymore. I can't swim twice a day, do well in school and be expected to have friends like a normal kid. And I don't even like it anymore. I feel like I have to win and if I don't, I feel sick like I'm gonna pass out. That can't be healthy. I just want to go to school and hang out with my friends and rent movies. I've already told coach Brian. He thinks I'm joking. I'm really not joking. I've had enough.

Outside Looking In

(speaking to a student)

I just want to thank you for being the only person in school to talk to me. You don't have to be my friend now or feel obligated to talk to me on a regular basis. I just wanted to let you know how much I appreciated what you did today. No one's ever done anything nice like that for me before. I won't take up much more of your time because I know if someone sees you talking to me you might not make any friends here. Because you look like someone who could probably make a lot of friends and I wouldn't want to stand in your way. You're a really nice person. I hope the kids like you as much as I do.

Commitments

(speaking to a friend)

Look I'm sorry I can't come to your party. I'm not doing it on purpose. I have to train. The nationals are coming up and I have to work really hard. Do you know how hard it was to make the team? I've been getting up every morning at 4:00 am to run for as long as I can remember. I'm not throwing it all away so I can come to your stupid party. I'm sorry. It's nothing personal. I have to eat and sleep and wake up early so I can train and win the meet next month or I won't get to go anywhere and then what will have been the point? *(beat)* You know you could be a little supportive.

Dreamer

(speaking to a friend)

I don't care what anyone says. I'm gonna be a star. I feel it in my bones. I've known it ever since I can remember. I can almost taste it. I know I have something that other people only wish they had. But I feel like if I'm gonna make a move I have to do it now. So I'm leaving. Please don't tell anyone. This is so important to me. I'm getting on the bus and not looking back. Next time you see me, I'll be on TV singing my heart out.

Like Mother Like Daughter

(speaking to her mother)

I don't want to be anything like you. When I have kids, they're gonna love me and respect me. And do you know why? Because I'm not gonna try to manipulate them or try to run their lives. I can't remember the last time I did something that you thought was worthy of your praise. As far as you're concerned, everything I do is not good enough. Well I don't need your approval any more. I'm not gonna spend the rest of my life trying to be someone I'm not just to make you happy. I'm outa here. Have a nice life, Mother.

Dropping Out

(speaking to a school counsellor)

I think I'm gonna take some time off. I mean I want to graduate, but I don't think I can do it this year. There's too much going on. I have some things to sort out and I can't do it here. I need to find some friends who understand me and can accept me for the person that I am. I'm not really finding anyone like that here. Everyone seems to want to be the same person. I can't do that. I need to be myself and not worry about what other people think of me. I gotta do that first. When I do that, I can come back and do this again.

I Think He Likes Me

(speaking to her sister)

So I think he likes me. But maybe he doesn't. I heard him tell his little sister Samantha that he thought I was cute. But it was far away. He might have said I was a brute. I don't know. He smiles at me when I walk by. That counts, doesn't it? Yesterday when I was waiting in line in the cafeteria he said "hey." Like you don't say "hey" to someone if you're indifferent about them right? Maybe tomorrow I'll say "hey" back.

Fat

(speaking to a team)

I can't eat that. It's too fattening. I don't eat anything that's fried or cooked in butter. I only eat raw food that doesn't have any preservatives. And coffee; I can have black coffee because it doesn't have any calories and because the caffeine helps me burn even more calories. *(looks at her watch)* And it's not even noon. Are you sure you want to eat that? I skip lunch now. I eat dry toast for breakfast and then I have to eat something in front of my mom at night so I pretend I'm full from lunch. Do you want my sandwich? At least it's peanut butter. It's a lot less fattening than that.

Silence

(speaking to a school counsellor)

Sometimes I set my alarm clock for 3:00 am so I can wake up and be surrounded by silence. I can think at 3:00 am. There's no one yelling at me or telling me what to do. It's just me. It's like I have an hour of clarity before I fall back asleep. I don't understand it really. I'm not sure why I do it but now it's a pattern and it's hard for me to break patterns. But the silence is so peaceful I don't think I'll ever want to give it up.

A Friend

(speaking to a guy)

I'm sorry I didn't return your phone calls. I haven't been sick. I've been at home because my mom's sick. She's dying. *(joking)* So you wanna see a movie? I'm sorry. It was nice to laugh though. Hey I drew you something. It's not much, but I wanted you to know that I was thinking about you…And if you want to call me sometime just to talk, that would be great. I can't be your girlfriend though. But I'd really love a friend right now.

The Report

(speaking to her teacher)

Mrs. Adams, I was just wondering if I could talk to you for a minute. I really don't feel comfortable presenting in front of the class. I mean I did my homework, I have it all typed up here *(shows her)* but I just really don't want to do it in front of the class. I have a really bad feeling in the pit of my stomach that if I present this speech in front of the class, I won't have any friends left. I'd love to present it for you sometime, but just not this afternoon, not in front of the class. I did my project on the pressures to buy coke in this school—not the drink. If I present this, no one will talk to me ever again. But I think you might like to hear it.

The Boyfriend

(speaking to a counsellor)

Yeah he hit me. Right here *(points to her chin)*. But it's not a big deal OK. I told him he was being a jerk and he hit me. But it's fine really. He loves me. He keeps telling me that. We're having a baby too. I'm three months pregnant. But don't tell anyone that. I haven't told my mom yet. She'll flip. But we're getting an apartment. He's gonna drop out of school to work so he can support us. So that shows that he loves us. And he's not gonna hit me anymore. So you don't have to report any of this. And if you do, I'll drop out of school too. I don't care about school anymore anyway. I'm gonna be a parent. I have to start thinking about that. That's more important than school.

Mirror, Mirror

(looking in the mirror, and applying make-up)

Mirror, mirror on the wall, who has the best Esprit bag of them all? *(smiles)* Me. Oh, what's that Susan, you wish you had my hair? But your hair's nice. It might need a few highlights but it definitely has major potential. What's that, Mom? You wish I spent more time studying than shopping? I wish you spent more time with me than with your stupid boyfriend. *(puts her bag down, looks up again at the mirror)* I'm not pretty, am I? I hate my life! I hate everything about this *(pointing at her body)*. My clothes, my make-up, my hair…who cares. No one cares. No one knows who I am. *(starts to smear her make-up)* This is me. This is who I am. I'm nothing but a poor little rich girl with a nice bag.

Abandoned

(speaking to the school counsellor)

My mom left yesterday. She said she wasn't coming back…I think it's my fault. I fool around too much and never help her around the house. She's been under a lot of stress lately and she couldn't take it. I just don't understand what I did wrong? If I knew, I'd fix it. I swear I would. My dad says she still loves us. I think he's lying. I can tell by the vein in his forehead. I think I'm gonna run away…or something.

The Divorce

(speaking to her mom)

It's not fair that I have to move! This stinks. This whole divorce stinks! It's all your fault and you know it. You cheated on Dad. You messed up and now we all have to suffer. Do you know what it's like to be a new kid at school halfway through the year? Everyone looks at you like you're some kind of leper. *(imitating)* "Oh I wonder what's wrong with her?" I'll have no friends and you don't even care!!! You're just a selfish, selfish person. *(beat)* Maybe I'll just tell the judge that I'm better off living with Dad.

The First Date

(speaking to a friend)

How do I look? Honest. Too much lipstick? Is my hair OK? Does this shirt go with these shoes? I'm so nervous I feel like my legs are gonna fall off. What do people talk about on first dates anyway? Should I talk about school? *(beat)* Of course not. Do I offer to pay? I'm confused. I don't know the first thing about what I'm supposed to do. He's so cute and I'm for sure gonna screw it all up.

Why Him?

(speaking to a friend)

I wish my mother's boyfriend would take a hike. I hate him. He thinks I have to answer to him. Why should I?!? He's just her stupid boyfriend. He's not my dad. My dad would never make me show him my purse when I got home from a party. It's like he's a prison guard or something. I wish he would just go away and leave me alone. If he moves in with us or, even worse, if my mom marries him, I'm leaving. I hate the guy.

Too Different

(speaking to her boyfriend)

You know I don't think this is gonna work out for us. We're just too different, you and I. I can't be with someone who doesn't care about anything else but himself. You know there are starving and homeless people all around the world and you don't even care. You didn't even care enough to watch the news when some of the major disasters of our time took place right in front of our faces. You were too busy hanging out with your friends or playing football to notice. I can't share my feelings and innermost thoughts with someone as selfish and immature as you.

Not the Movies

(speaking to a friend)

Why can't it be like the movies? When some girl dates a lot of guys in the movies it's a romantic comedy about a girl who's misunderstood and still looking for Mr. Right. She's always cute and so well liked and just waiting to be saved by some Hollywood hottie. But in real life, if you're a girl who's dated a lot of guys all of whom know each other, you're a slut. *(beat)* Where's the Hollywood ending there?

Valedictorian

(making the valedictory address at graduation)

So I'm here, grade 12 graduation, and I've managed to get through high school without eating a single cafeteria quesadilla and everyone knows how hard that is. For those of you who don't get the joke, it's hard to get around eating the quesadillas in this school because they're one of three constant staples in our fine school eatery. But enough about quesadillas; there's something more pending I want to spend my five minutes of fame discussing. For most this was a great year. A year filled with accomplishments spanning athletic victories to school productions and provincial debating awards. Some of us went on field trips to see fantastic plays, others went skiing in Banff or took a whirlwind trip through Europe with memories that will last a lifetime. And as spectacular as this year might appear to the outside observer, there's one student who didn't get to experience any of the things that I've just mentioned. That student is Melody Sins. Some of you might remember Melody. She was in our grade 11 year. She had pretty blond hair and glasses and aside from being painfully shy was one of the nicest people I've ever had the pleasure of knowing. The reason why Melody didn't get to experience any of the great things that we experienced this year is because she's no longer with us and I don't mean she's no longer a student at our school anymore but she's simply not anymore. Melody took her own life over the summer. She felt she had no friends. She felt she was not worthy of doing all the super things we all had the opportunity to do this year. I'm sure everyone here will agree that that's simply not true. *(gaining composure)* When we embark on our new lives outside of high school following fulfilling careers, starting families and doing all the exciting things we ought to do during our lifetimes, please never forget Melody. Even if you never spoke to her or noticed her, she should be a part of you for the rest of your life because she deserved to be here too but because of our indifference and frivolous nature as teenagers, without meaning to or wanting to we all contributed to her not being here. Let's make sure that as adults we make things right by always remembering a girl who said so little but taught us all so much.

Skin Deep

(speaking to a guidance counsellor)

It doesn't really hurt that bad. *(lifting her long sleeve shirt to expose bandages on her arms)* I only cut myself in places where people can't see. Then I cover it up so I can't see. *(pulls down her sleeve)* It's really not that bad. I don't know why you people are making such a big deal about it. I'm sure I'm not the only student in this school that cuts herself. You should spend your time on some of the school's bigger problems like drugs. There are a lot of drugs in this school you know. *(beat)* I just hate it here. This place is such a dive. The only people who enjoy going here are the pretty girls who date the football players. It's such an 80's cliché. It's ridiculous. *(beat)* Sometimes I feel like I'm gonna suffocate. I look around in science class and it's like a video with no sound; I can see people looking at me and laughing at me but I can't hear it. If I can't hear it maybe it doesn't exist. Maybe it's just in my head.

Power Trip

(speaking to a classmate)

What did you just say to me?!? What makes you think you can talk to me? You're an idiot. No! You can't be my partner. I'd rather die. Are you for real? What in the world would ever make you think that I would pair up with such a reject like you? You're a joke. I can't believe you had the guts to come over here. You're such a loser. Now get away before people see me talking to you. Why don't you ask that geek over there to be your partner? Surprisingly she looks like no one's asked her yet. Get lost, will you? *(to another student)* Hey, do you have a partner yet?

The Plot

(speaking to a friend in the bathroom)

I can't believe I got a zit on the day of the dance. Well I'm not going to the dance with a zit on my nose. Forget that. *(beat)* What if Tyler ends up with someone else tonight? Who am I kidding, of course he's gonna end up with someone else. AHHH I'm so angry! Why did this have to happen to me? I'm sure Tiffany's gonna be all over him when she sees I'm not there. *(beat)* Listen, you have to make sure that Tiffany doesn't go near my boyfriend at the dance tonight—you hear?!? Do whatever you have to do to keep that tart away from him. I give you permission to spill punch on her, lock her in the bathroom, trip her, threaten her, beat her up, run over her with your car if you have to; just do whatever! Keep her away from Tyler!

Broke

(speaking to her mother)

Mom, can I talk to you please? I know we don't have a lot of money right now and that you work really hard and you're doing your best and I'm really sorry but I have to ask you for something. I need new clothes, Mom. The kids at school, they're really mean when kids don't wear the right clothes. They don't laugh at you or call you names but they exclude you and pretend that you're not there. No one's wearing the same jeans that they wore last year. Everyone's wearing new clothes and the girls in my class are wearing these camisoles that don't look like they're too expensive. I know I'm not allowed to get a job because I have to baby-sit Benny when you're working but I'll do extra things around the house and maybe I could deliver flyers on Saturday morning and take Benny with me. *(beat)* Mom. You have to help me. No one talks to me at school. I have to get new clothes.

The Invitation

(speaking to a classmate)

Oh I love your top! Where did you get it? You have such great taste. I love all your clothes. Hey did you wanna hang out with us at lunch today? We think you're really cute and smart and would love to hang out with you. *(pointing)* We sit over there by the drink machine. You're welcome to join us and then you can tell us all about where you shop for clothes. Maybe we could all go shopping on Saturday and then go to a movie or dinner after. It'll be fun. You're so nice. We always talk about how much we like you. *(beat)* But when you come for lunch don't bring Stacey; no offence but we don't really like her. She's a little bit of an oddball. You understand, right?

DRAMATIC MONOLOGUES FOR YOUNG MEN

Murder

(speaking to an officer, wearing a white shirt stained in blood, hands stained as well)

I'd like to turn myself in. I killed someone. My dad. He was a drunk with a quick hand and he swung it for the last time at my little sister, who I think someone should go check on because she looked pretty bad where I left her. Her head hit the kitchen table. I think she's unconscious. She's still breathing though. My mom you won't find. I think she's gone to kill herself. I gathered that from the note she left on the kitchen table that said "I'm going to kill myself." I have no remorse. I'm not sorry for what I've done. I'm no longer a minor. I want to be locked up somewhere for a very long time. And I don't want any visitors, except my sister when she feels better. She was unconscious before I killed him so she played no part at all in this murder. My mother wasn't home either. If you find her alive, I don't want to see her. She's dead to me now. I left the gun on the kitchen counter because I didn't want to walk down the street holding a gun and scaring people. You'll find my finger prints on it and my dead father beside that and my unconscious sister not too far off from him. *(showing him his thumb)* Do you need my prints?

The Interview

(wearing a suit and tie and looking in the mirror and practicing for a job interview)

(stretching out his hand) Hi Mr. Donovan, I'm Wilson Stewart. I don't know if you remember me, I used to kiss your son in the boys' bathroom at Concordia. *(beat)* Hi Mr. Donovan, I'm Wilson Stewart. I don't know if you remember me, I used to play soccer with your son Franky; we used to do it in the back of your Oldsmobile. *(beat)* Hi Mr. Donovan, I'm Wilson Stewart; I hope you don't remember me. *(beat)* Hi Mr. Donovan, it's nice to see you again; are you still a homophobic bastard? *(beat)* Hi Mr. Donovan, I've been really looking forward to seeing you again. How's Franky? *(beat)* Hi Mr. Donovan…*(takes a good look in the mirror, takes off his tie)*.

The Date

(a geeky fellow with a pocket protector)

(To a girl) I cut this flower for you. *(smiles)* It's pretty like you. I was wondering if you wanted to go out sometime. I'll pay for dinner. My dad gave me $50.00 just last weekend to detail his car. I saved it so I could take you somewhere nice. We can go see a movie too if you'd like. *(beat)* If you don't want to see a movie we can take a walk in the park. *(beat)* If you don't have time because you have homework to do, I can help you with your homework. I can do your homework, for free this time. Mine's all done. I finished it after school in the cafeteria so I would have time to go home, shower, get changed, pick this flower and come out here and find you so I could take you somewhere nice. *(beat)* That's OK, I'll invest my $50.00. One day you'll remember this and wish you went out with me.

Squeegee Kid

(trying to stop cars)

Can I wash your windshield... Jerk. Can I wash your... Fat Ass. Can I... Thanks. *(washes windshield)* Hey! Hey! Ahh. This sucks. *(puts squeegee down, takes off hat and puts hat out in front of him)*. I'm really hungry, sir. Do you think you could spare a dollar? Fifty cents? A quarter! Hi man, I'm really hungry do you think you could...thanks! *(looks in hat)* A quarter, great. *(thinks it over, takes quarter out of hat)*. Hey man, can I buy a smoke?

The Mistake

(speaking to his grandmother)

(Kneeling, in front of an imaginary wheelchair) Grandma...I need to tell you something. I won't be around anymore. I'm going away. I got this scholarship to go to university... No I didn't. I did something bad, Grandma, and I have to go away. I'm sorry. But I'm gonna be fine and I'm gonna make you proud of me someday... just not today. So I need you to understand that I won't be around to visit you anymore. But I'm gonna write you letters, Grandma, and the nurse said she's gonna read them to you, OK? I'm really sorry, Grandma. I screwed up. I really screwed up this time.

Drunk Driving

(speaking to an officer)

Is she dead? I was driving the car. I thought I was OK to drive because out of the entire group I drank the least. I only had three beers and I didn't smoke any weed. I was supposed to drive everyone home. They trusted me to drive them home. Did I hit a tree? Please tell me I hit a tree? How many people died? Am I going to jail? Can I call my parents? Can I please phone my parents?

Anger

(speaking to his girlfriend)

Look I'm sorry I hit you. I've said I'm sorry so many times I'm beginning to slur...I'll never hit you again. *(beat)* Hit me. Go ahead and hit me. It'll make you feel better. Hell it'll make me feel better. Look I'm not an asshole! You're not going to make me out to be an asshole because I hit you. Once. I hit you once! And you were really ticking me off.

Starting Over

(speaking to a friend)

I sometimes think it would be easier if I weren't around anymore. Like I'm not thinking about killing myself or anything like that, but I would like to disappear if I could. Like be lost and not found again. I think of those people in the witness protection program and how awesome it would be to reinvent myself, completely. Just become another person. I get this urge in the middle of the night to get in my car and drive away...somewhere. It would be like killing myself and being reborn. I've gotten as far as the driveway in my pyjamas and caught myself holding the door handle and picturing a new life unfolding.

The First Time

(speaking to a girl)

I've never done this before. I feel really nervous. I bought some protection. I think I got the right one, but I'm not sure. It's important to have the right one. That's what I've been told. Some guys practice putting this on at home. I didn't. I kinda wish I did. If you don't want to do this, I'm really OK with that. I'm very OK with that. Have you done this before? I'm sure you've done this before. Have I mentioned I haven't done this before.

Caught

(speaking to a police officer)

Like I'm the only one in the school who sells drugs. Give me a break. Where are the rest of the "dealers"? *(beat)* I only sell marijuana, and not even a lot of it. I steal it from my older brother. I'm more afraid of him than you, so please don't tell anyone I took his drugs. He thinks one of his friends is ripping him off and I'd like to leave it that way. He's waiting for proof so he can beat him with a tire wrench. Get my drift? There are kids in this school that sell coke, meth, acid, you name it. And they don't steal it from their brother. They have suppliers that have suppliers. I don't know why I'm here.

Part-time Work

(speaking to his boss)

No. I won't do it. Fire me. I can't work next weekend. I have to study for my math test. If I don't, I fail. Like I fail high school and I don't get to graduate. What do you care? As long as you have someone peeling potatoes and washing dishes, it doesn't make a difference to you. One lousy weekend. When I asked you a week ago, you said "yes." So why is it "no" now? I quit. Find someone else to work this weekend.

Seating Plan

(speaking to a teacher)

He deserved it. I'd do it again. The kid's annoying. Every stinking day he has some stupid story to tell about some holiday he took with his parents to Cuba or The Netherlands. Someone needed to clock him right in the middle of the face to shut him up. Tomorrow, can I sit somewhere else? Like over there beside the kid who never talks. I could sit there and be very happy.

The STD

(speaking to his doctor and holding two pieces of paper)

What do you mean I have gonorrhea? What the hell is that? *(looking at one of his papers)* And what the hell is this? Contact tracing?!? You want to know everyone I've ever been with? *(mortified)* Are they gonna know that I gave it to them? I'm gonna die. No one is ever going to come near me again. I'm fifteen. Never is a very long time. *(looking at second piece of paper)* And what the hell is this? Are these antibiotics gonna make this go away? Is this ever gonna go away?!? When will the burning stop, doc? Oh forget it. My life is over.

Déjà Vu

(speaking to a girl)

That's OK, there's nothing you can say to me that I haven't already heard before. It's clear you don't want to date me. That's cool. I didn't expect that someone like you would want to hang out with someone like me anyway. I just thought I would try, I guess. It would have been nice to date someone as pretty as you but I understand you probably get better offers all the time. Anyway, see you around.

The Girlfriend

(talking to his best friend)

It's just that ever since you started hanging out with Curtis we don't spend a lot of time together anymore. I mean don't get me wrong, I think it's great you have a boyfriend. I think it's awesome you have a boyfriend, but I guess I thought we would still be able to hang out and shoot hoops and do the things we've always done and...we haven't. I've been left out of everything the two of you do and I'm starting to feel rejected. When you're out having all this fun, what am I supposed to do?

Scalper

(scalping tickets outside a sporting event)

Hey aren't you in my little brother's grade? I know you. Hey you wanna buy a couple of tickets? It's all sold out you know. They're only fifty each. With a price like that... *(beat)* How could you not want to buy them at that price? No one anywhere around here has the same deal going. What's the matter, you don't like hockey? Look twerp. I said fifty bucks. It's no longer optional. I have tickets and you have money so let's get this over with before I have to kick the crap out of you. I'm not kidding, OK? Hand over the cash or I'll look for it myself! Do you have a death wish or something?!? *(pulls out a pocket knife)*. Open your wallet or I'll slice you.

Instigator

(speaking to a teacher)

Why do I get a detention?!? I'm the one with the black eye. Didn't you see that kid hit me? I don't know what his problem is. I was just joking around. Jeez. He takes everything so personally. Would he rather we just ignored him? He should be happy that we include him at all. He's such a loser. We're just trying to be nice to him. It's not my fault he doesn't have any friends. I don't know why you're giving me the detention. *(pointing)* That stupid kid swinging his fist should be punished. I didn't hit'im; I was just teasing him. What's the big deal anyway?

Hockey Dad

(speaking to his father)

Enough, OK! I've had enough, Dad! Stop it! Stop yelling at me at my games. It's humiliating. I'm terrified out there because I'm try-ing not to mess up so you won't start screaming from the stands like some lunatic. Can't you see that everyone is looking at you funny?!?! I'm not having any fun! I'm gonna quit! I hate hockey! I hate everything about it. We're not spending any quality time together like the other kids are with their dads. What's the point? It's supposed to be a game, isn't it? Why can't you just groan or cheer like the other parents do? I hate this. I hate the way you treat me. I hate that you think I have to be perfect all the time. I hate that I'll never live up to your standards. I hate you!

Hall Monitor

(speaking to his teacher)

No I can't be the hall monitor. Are you crazy? What, you want me to rat on other kids, preferably the kind that retaliate after school? No thank you. Ask someone else to be your hall monitor. And you're not going to find any takers by the way. Kids wanna hang out at lunch time. They wanna talk on their cell phones, walk to 7-Eleven or smoke cigarettes across the street. What they don't wanna be doing is wearing pocket protectors in the hallway taking notes of who's saying what. I might as well paint a big bull's eye on my face. That way kids will know who to kick the crap out of after school. You people can't be serious that you're thinking students are going to police students. Hire a parent. Buy a video camera but leave me out of it!

Chapter 6: **The Audition! Slating and more**

If you've got something to say, say it, and think well of yourself while you're learning to say it better.

—David Mamet from his book *True and False: Heresy and Common Sense for the Actor*

Most drama teachers will tell you that they teach monologues in order to prepare students for audition situations. And yet many drama teachers rush through their "audition" unit haphazardly throwing it in somewhere towards the end of the year when all audition opportunities have already passed! Why is this?

We spend the better half of the school year allowing students to master concepts like improvisation and scene work but spend very little time on the component of acting that leaves an actor feeling the most vulnerable and alone. And when students are left to their own devices to find monologues for audition purposes, they often select pieces that they don't understand, are too long, are not age appropriate or all of the above.

This chapter will teach you that there really isn't much to preparing students for a successful audition or running one for that matter. The key is to be organized and have lots of student helpers!

THE IMPORTANCE OF STAGE MANAGERS

It wasn't until after directing my first major production in a middle school that I realized I needed to enlist students to perform stage managerial duties that otherwise left me run off my feet. Simple things we as teachers take for granted, like time we spend photocopying scripts, is time better spent directing students and analysing scripts. If you're a do-it-all kind of drama educator, please take the following advice to heart: **don't do anything a student can do for you.** Students obviously can't teach your class or direct your plays, but they certainly can help by photocopying, placing announcements in the school office and making cast lists on the computer.

If students are earning a credit for your school's major production, you can easily assign 2 – 4 students to stage manage (and perhaps have them also double as assistant directors), taking care of all your production jobs and freeing up your time so you can do what students really need you to do, and that's direct.

Here is a list of some production duties that your student stage managers can perform:

1. **Daily announcements:** When you nail down a date for your auditions, your student SMs can put together a brief announcement stating the time and date of the audition; they can then submit the announcement to the school office making sure it's announced every day for at least two weeks.

2. **Slating:** Because some students who audition might not know how to slate, have your SMs create a poster, stating the following, to be posted outside the theatre or audition room on the day of the audition.

ATTENTION ACTORS

All students will be asked to slate on stage prior to performing their monologues.

Slating consists of:

STATING YOUR NAME

"Hi my name's _____"

STATING YOUR PIECES IN ORDER

"I'll be performing two monologues, one comic and one dramatic. The first monologue is entitled

_____

and it's written by_____

and the second is entitled _____

and it's written by _____."

NB. After slating, set up for your monologues using mime boxes found on either side of the stage (if needed). After performing your piece, return any mime boxes to where you found them. Good luck!

3. **Keeping the clock:** During auditions, make sure your SMs keep you on time. If you have 40 – 60 fifteen-minute auditions over the course of three days, it's imperative that you keep it moving! Have one student SM seated beside you reminding you of the time while another knocks on the door when your time is up. This works great because it also helps the actors understand that every student is getting equal time.

4. **Call backs:** If you want to spend more time with students you can call them back at a later date to see more of their work. After deciding who gets called back, have your SMs post a call back list or have them phone students at home using information gathered from their **contact/information sheets** (see below).

5. **Cast lists:** When a cast has been decided upon, have student SMs type up a cast list and post it outside the theatre. The cast list should be announced the day after call backs.

6. **Photocopying:** Have your SMs take care of photocopying all scripts and typed material (letters to parents, costume and make-up information, etc.), having the material ready to hand out immediately after the cast list has been posted.

7. **Sign-up sheet:** After deciding when and where you want to hold the auditions, you need to decide how much time you require for each audition. Anywhere from 10 – 20 minutes is appropriate for high school.

8. **Contact/information sheet:** Have students prepare a contact sheet where students can write down their name, phone number, grade and any other pertinent information. Information you wish to gather on your contact sheet may include:

- Drama experience: list plays and classes
- Availability: what days are you not available?
- Preference in role: lead, cameo?
- Special talents: gymnastics, dancing, musical instruments
- Production duties of interest: painting, props, costumes, make-up, etc.

Contact sheets will differ from show to show depending on what you're looking for in your cast. These are just some general ideas to get you started.

9. **Monologue cheat sheet:** If you know you'll be auditioning students who have little or no experience working with monologues, have your students mail the following **Monologue cheat sheet** to new students:

Monologue Cheat Sheet

Comic

(Speaking to your teacher, Mr. Richards)

Look Mr. Richards; I know I shouldn't have put gum on your chair...but it was funny. Everyone said it was funny. *(beat)* I can't get a detention. My mom says if I get one more detention I'm gonna have to switch to kitchen duty. Do you know what kitchen duty is Mr. Richards? I have five siblings, two parents, one grandmother and a dog. Kitchen duty is what they make you do in hell. I have to wash all the dishes after every meal, sweep the floor and mop. But it's not really mopping. Mopping is what normal people do. My mom insists on cleaning the floor with a sponge! Who does that? I can't be on kitchen duty.

Dramatic

(speaking to the school counsellor)

My mom left yesterday. She said she wasn't coming back...I think it's my fault. I fool around too much and never help her around the house. She's been under a lot of stress lately and she couldn't take it. I just don't understand what I did wrong? If I knew, I'd fix it. I swear I would. My dad says she still loves us. I think he's lying. I can tell by the vein in his forehead. I think I'm gonna run away...or something.

Helpful hints in preparing your audition

1. Never play an emotion. You can't play "angry"; don't even try. Instead, decide what your character wants from the other character and play that action. Does your character want someone to listen to him/her? Does your character want a break?

2. Always place the (imaginary) person you are speaking to in front of you and above the director's table.

3. Never look at the director when you are presenting. When rehearsing in front of your teacher, friends or family, ignore them. They are simply watching you deal with someone else. Imagine a fourth wall directly in front of your audience.

4. Have fun!

THE DIRECTOR'S ROLE

While your students are running around getting ready for the big day, you should be making yourself available to students who need help with their monologues or teaching your drama students how to **slate** during class time.

Teaching students to slate

Have students perform the following tasks in front of the class:

- Walk into the room and smile at the director(s)
- Go up onto the stage (downstage centre)
- Slate—stating their name and title(s) of their piece(s)
- Set up for their monologue
- Say the first and last line of their monologue
- Put away any set pieces
- Smile, say thank you and exit.

If students are performing more than one piece they need to take a moment to set up the second monologue (students should be efficient but not rush) and repeat what they did with the first piece.

Pre-audition tips

Before students slate point out the following things to them:

1. **Don't look at the directors!** The director is not the actor's scene partner. The actor should place person B directly over the heads of the directors. Don't assume that students paid attention to the helpful hints on your **Monologue Cheat Sheet**; if they're nervous they're bound to forget a few things.

2. **They may be interrupted:** Prepare students for the prospect that they may be stopped to be given direction and then asked to start again. Without this warning, students who have never auditioned before may take your interjections as a sign of failure and give up halfway through the audition.

3. **Remind students to slate:** Even though there is a sign out-side the theatre telling students to slate, your high school

play is not a Hollywood cattle call. Remind students to introduce themselves and state the titles of their pieces in order.
Also take this opportunity to remind students where they can
find mime boxes.

4. **Tell students where you want them to stand:** Some directors are firm that students should be 10 feet away from the
director's table. You can do whatever best suits you. In high
school, I find that projection is a main casting factor; therefore I tend to start off at the director's table and slowly move
towards the back of the theatre where I stand to gauge volume. Students tend to project more if they know the director
is at the back of the theatre.

5. **Everyone gets equal time:** Inform students that the
audition will be brief and if you need to see more they
will be called back.

6. **Relax and do your best:** Take some of the pressure off your
aspiring thespians by smiling and genuinely wishing them
luck. Some students physically shake during auditions and
I've seen more than a few kids cry over the years. It takes a lot
of guts for them to be there. Let's make this a self-esteem
booster and not a downer for these kids. Teachers should not
be standoffish towards students in the spirit of replicating a
professional audition situation. I've auditioned for professional theatres and I've never been greeted with aloofness by a
director or treated like a number. While we want to run our
auditions as professionally as possible, we can not forget that
as teachers of theatre we have a responsibility to model
the etiquette we expect our students to adhere to come
rehearsal time.

7. **Take your time:** Remind students to take a deep breath and
begin when they're ready and take a few moments before
breaking out of character at the end of the monologue.
Nervousness often causes young actors to rush through their
pieces. If you feel a student is rushing, stop them and tell
them to begin again but this time taking their time and
savouring every moment they have on stage.

8. **Ask students if they have any questions:** Give students the opportunity to ask you questions about the show, their monologue or their audition. This gives you a chance to informally meet students but also breaks the ice and helps students feel more at ease.

9. **Rehearsals!** It doesn't matter how brilliant a student is or how lovely they are to work with. If they're on every sports team there is, they're probably not an ideal candidate for the lead in your school musical. Don't make deals with students. **All students are expected to attend all rehearsals.** Students who are over-programmed and miss rehearsals will only create animosity among the cast who will feel (and rightly so) that there is preferential treatment given to certain students.

10. **Review contact sheet:** Don't wait until students have left to review their **contact/information sheet.** Review it during the audition so if you have any questions you can have them answered while the student is in front of you.

Directing

Before the auditions even start you should have a clear idea of what you're looking for in each actor you want to cast. Generally you're probably looking for students who are easy to work with, polite and chipper, hard workers, have strong voices and are easily directed. You also might have a certain prototype in your mind of how each character should look on stage. While that might be the case, keep an open mind because often students give you something other than what you're looking for but with a little imagination you'll sometimes find that what they're giving you works even better than what you originally anticipated!

When auditioning, allow students to show you what they've prepared before giving them things to work on. Keep in mind that you have a limited amount of time so stick with the basics:

1. Can you hear them from the back of the theatre?

2. Are they directable? If you ask them to try a different action can they change what they originally prepared to include your ideas and suggestions?

3. If necessary can they change their character's **effort action, centre or status?**

4. Do they become frustrated or defensive when you ask them to try something new?

5. Do they seem prepared, willing to work hard and of course available for your scheduled rehearsals?

Being a cheerleader

As mentioned before, it takes a great deal of guts for students to get up on that stage in an audition situation. Auditioning makes even the most seasoned of actors nauseous. Encourage students before they begin, while you're directing them and when they leave. And remember, you are not working with professionals but high school students trying their best under extreme pressure. Encourage them! Encourage them! Encourage them!

Always finding room in the inn

In my shows no one is left behind and I highly encourage you to consider doing the same. If there is no part, make one. How about assistant stage manager, head of props, make-up, costumes, poster designer, set designer or house manager, to name but a few. There is really no excuse to turn kids away from the theatre. The jobs associated with a major production are endless. Don't pass up an opportunity to make your production the best it can be by enlisting the help of as many enthusiastic students as possible. Why not have the biggest chorus your school has ever seen!

Make a list of each and every job that needs to be filled and have students sign up for jobs they would like to perform, encouraging them to also take on leadership roles where you feel it's appropriate. A production has so many intricate details that culminate in its success. Student actors also need to realize how many competent people it takes to mount a show. Having numerous students involved in the major production builds community in your school and for some drama teachers, that's why they direct plays in the first place!

The Audition Survival Kit

The importance of stage managers

- Don't do anything a student can do for you.

- Student stage managers can:

  1. Make daily announcements

  2. Make informative posters on **slating**

  3. Keep the clock

  4. Make phone calls for **call backs**

  5. Post **cast lists**

  6. Photocopy

  7. Make a **sign-up sheet** for auditions

  8. Make a **contact/information sheet**

  9. Mail a **monologue cheat sheet** to new students

The Director's Role

- Teach students to slate in class

- Give students pre-audition tips like:

  1. Don't look at the directors

  2. You may be interrupted

  3. Remember to slate

  4. Where to stand

5.   Everyone gets equal time

6.   Relax and do your best

7.   Take your time

8.   Feel free to ask questions

9.   All students are expected to attend all rehearsals

10. Reviewing contact sheet

■ Direct students during auditions paying particular attention to:

1.   Volume

2.   If students are directable

3.   Can they change effort **actions, centres and status** on demand?

4.   Do they become frustrated when asked to try something new?

5.   Do they seem prepared, willing to work hard and available for rehearsals?

■ Be a cheerleader

■ Always find room in the inn

Chapter 7: Making an evening of it

Tell a story worth telling.

—Per Brask

So now that you have monologues, why limit them to the audition room? Share them. Allow your students the pleasure of performing the monologues they've worked so hard to create in an easy-to-produce evening of monologues. You will love this low-key event and once you get started it will quickly become an annual event in your school and something that your students will eagerly anticipate year after year. An evening of monologues doesn't involve big budgets (in fact if you do it right, no budget) and it allows each student an opportunity to really command the stage on their own, something most students otherwise *never* have the opportunity to do, not even if they're the lead in the school play.

In an evening of monologues, there are no overwhelming sets or ridiculous wigs distracting the audience from what is really important on that stage and that's of course your wonderful students. Every student gets to be a lead for one evening! Where on earth would you ever find a play like that?

CREATING AN EVENING OF MONOLOGUES

Your task is simple. Find the students. They can be students you teach during the regular timetable or students you direct in your lunch or after-school drama club. I've done both. When I first started teaching drama in a middle school, all our plays and performances were extra-curricular. My first monologue evening was an extra-curricular activity in a high school when I was teaching drama part-time. Later, when I ran an entire high school Drama department, I made it mandatory for all my performance students to participate in an evening of monologues in the first semester of the year. It took place after our basic acting unit had been completed and, along with giving students a venue to display the acting techniques they had learned in class, it gave each and student an opportunity to shine on stage alone.

Depending on your program you can decide how many students you want to participate in your evening of monologues and how you want to set it up. Remember to keep the monologues short, mixing up the comic and dramatic pieces in order to add variation to the evening. A monologue evening should be short and sweet. Anywhere from 30 – 60 minutes is acceptable and if you are showcasing different classes, it's advisable to have an intermission. I would recommend showcasing the grade 9 and 10 students and then break before continuing with the grade 11 and 12 students. You can also draw which classes go first or last if it seems to be an issue with your students. If you choose to have all your drama classes perform, I wouldn't recommend you mix up the grade levels (for example have a grade 9 student perform followed by a grade 12 student) because then you have to schedule rehearsals outside of class time in order to get all your grade levels together for one rehearsal time. That can be very tricky!

DIRECTING

Since your monologues have already been directed in your monologue unit, other than a couple of 2-hour rehearsals to settle production issues, you're well on your way! Note that if you have more than one class performing, you need to have two 2-hour rehearsals for **each** group.

Rehearsal #1: 2 Hours

You'll need to set up 3 spotlights: downstage right (DR), downstage centre (DC) and downstage left (DL). Number the spots 1, 2, and 3 (see Figure 1 below) and then give every student in the class a number based on how many students are in the class. For instance, if there are 15 students in the class, you will need to number the class 1-15. The first student (student assigned #1 of 15) will be in spot 1 (DC), the second student will be in spot 2 (DR) and the third student will be in spot 3 (DL). The fourth student will be in spot 1 again and the pattern continues (1,2,3) for the rest of the class.

Ask students to divide themselves into two equal groups for backstage purposes. Students who are performing in the downstage right (DR) spotlight should be positioned backstage right. Students performing in the downstage left (DL) spotlight should be positioned backstage left and students performing downstage centre can be on either side of the backstage area.

Figure 1:

UR	US	UL
R	C	L
DR spot 2	DC spot 1	DL spot 3

Ask students to bring their costumes and props to both rehearsals, locking them in their lockers for safekeeping when they are not being utilized. Assign a student stage manager to make a list of who is where backstage and also to ensure that there are three mime boxes on either side of the backstage area for students to use as set pieces if needed.

When you've determined who should be where, explain to students that there will be a **cross fade** between the monologues. What this means is when the lights are slowly fading on the actor who has just performed his monologue, the lights are slowly coming up on the next performer.

Sometimes audiences applaud loudly between monologues. Have the student lighting technician lengthen the timing of the cross fade, taking longer for the next performer's light to be at full, and timing it so that the lights go up to full immediately after the audience has quieted down. Audiences will keep it brief when they see the next performer is ready to go whereas a blackout invites an undetermined amount of applause and this lengthens the duration of the show considerably.

After explaining to the students how the lighting will work, tell them you will be performing a **Cue to Cue**. A Cue to Cue or what I sometimes call a **First Line Last Line** requires students to **hit their mark** (go where they need to go on stage), say the first line of their piece, the last line of their piece and exit. This is done so students can see who is before and after them and deal with any complications resulting from backstage confusion. In the professional theatre and during your technical rehearsals for school productions, Cue to Cues are used to design light and sound cues, but for the Cue to Cue is used to orient and organize the actors.

One of the things students need to do is commit to memory the last line of the student before them in the show's running order. They need to do this because students will set up for their monologue during the previous performer's last line. And because students should have no more than one mime box and one prop to carry on to the stage, set-up should literally take seconds.

Allow students an opportunity to conference with each other, committing to memory their classmate's last line and putting their things in order for a **First Line Last Line**. Make sure that your student SM has recorded the running order of the show and everyone's last line for the lighting technicians. When your students are ready, have your student SM say "slow fade to black" cueing student #1 to set up in spot 1 (figure 1) and then "lights up" cueing student #1 to say her first and last line. When student #2 hears the beginning of student #1's last line he needs to quickly get into spot 2. In some cases you may find that students will need to set up on the second last line but not sooner. When the SM says "cross fade," student #2 should say his first and last line and the pattern continues for the rest of the cast. You will not require stage lights for this rehearsal. Stage lights will be used in the second rehearsal.

At the end of the **First Line Last Line**, invite students to sit along the downstage area of the stage for your **director's notes**. This is your opportunity to give students any direction you wish to give them regarding theatrical and production matters. Make sure to tell students that even before the light starts coming up on them, they should be in character and ready to go and when they have delivered their last line, they need to stay in the moment until they are in a complete blackout. Have students count to five after they think they are in a blackout and then move. Novice students will find it difficult to recognize when the light is at full or when they are in a complete blackout. In rehearsal #2 the lighting technicians will go through the difference between a faded light and a blackout and demonstrate how bright the lights need to get before students begin their monologue.

You should also **block** or **stage** (direct the actors' movements on stage) the bows in the first rehearsal. I prefer one clean line downstage centre. Have students go backstage and come out forming a line that, depending on the number of students you have, spans the centre or entire downstage area. Assign a reliable student to stand in the middle of the line and cue the class to bow. When the line is formed, have everyone look to the student in the center. She will discreetly look to her right, then her left and then out to the audience. When she looks out to the audience, that's everyone's cue to slowly bow together. You can verbally run the class through your **magic bowing trick** by saying "right, left, bow" and repeating this until students feel comfortable with the routine and timing. If the bow looks too fast, have students do it again in slow motion. Repeat until you are happy with the end result.

Rehearsal #2: 2 Hours

Rehearsal #2 will consist of the following:

- Have the stage managers make sure everyone is where they need to be backstage and that everyone knows the last or second last line of the person before them.

- Have the lighting technicians demonstrate the blackouts and the cross fades to the cast, who should sit in the audience to get the full effect. Students should also be given the opportunity to stand in the various spotlights to better understand when the lights are at full and when they are in a complete blackout.

- If you haven't already done so, assign a student to run the **warm-up** on the day of the performance; this could be your SM.

- Do a **Cue to Cue** or **First Line Last Line** using the stage lights.

- Ask students if there are any difficulties or concerns regarding the lights (i.e., can they see where they're going in order to get to their mark?) Most often your lighting technicians or stage managers will need to place glow tape on the floor in certain areas so students can see where they are going.

- Run a full technical dress rehearsal whereby students say their entire monologues without being interrupted by you, the SM or the lighting technicians.

- Give students your **director's notes** on what needs to be cleaned up by show time. You can give both individual notes and group notes. To save time you might want to give group notes verbally to the entire group and then give students their individual notes written on pieces of paper just for them. The best way to do this is to have a piece of paper for every student in the class already labelled (e.g., Jenny) on your director's table before the run begins.

- Encourage students to give their *notes.* A good idea is to have a piece of paper taped on either side of the backstage area titled **"Student Notes"** and have students write down any problems, suggestions or concerns they might have during the run. At the end of the rehearsal, have the SM take down the pieces of paper and together with your cast, address student concerns during **student notes** which will take place after your notes. This eliminates students talking to each other during rehearsal or feeling they need to disrupt the run to talk to you. If students know they will be heard at some point, they will wait patiently until it is their turn to share their concerns, ideas and suggestions.

LIGHTING

If you don't have a design background, find someone in the school who knows how to hang and focus lights. If your school doesn't have stage lights, consider borrowing from another school. You could rent but stage lights can be pricey. The advantage of renting, however, is that you can get the technician to hang and focus your lights for you. If you pay for this service once, taking notes and training a couple of keen students along with you, you can forgo the fee next time and simply pay the cost of renting.

Most school theatres will have a selection of **ellipsoidal spotlights** and **fresnel floodlights** (see figure 2) to work with. An Ellipsoidal spotlight allows you to create hard and soft edges and control the size of the spot quite easily. Fresnel (pronounced *fernél*) floodlights do what they say, they flood a pool of light. You can control the light however by using **barn doors** that attach to the front of the instrument allowing you to adjust the light by opening and closing the doors.

Figure 2

Ellipsoidal spotlight

Fresnel floodlight with barn doors

You will require a total of 9 lights, 3 for each area that needs to be illuminated. If your school has a well-stocked theatre and technical booth and you have access to more lights, then great! But if you need to borrow or rent, 9 will give you a very nice effect.

Important things to remember when designing your lights:

- Don't use coloured gels unless you have a professional helping you. While gels can enhance a certain mood, used incorrectly they can wash out actors or cast darkness. And because your monologues are both comedic and dramatic, you'll need to create light that will complement everyone's piece.

- Make sure the spot is tight and that there are three separate spots that don't overlap (see figure 1).

- Have your technicians make an X with glow tape in the centre of each spot so that students know where their **mark** is.

Some theatres have sophisticated lighting boards that can program lights while others have less sophisticated manual boards. They both do the same job in the end. Have students make a 10 count (count to 10) to complete each cross fade.

If your SM is not performing in the show, she can sit in the booth and **call the show**, alerting the technicians when they should change the lights. A stage manager can say "stand by" a couple of lines before the cue to change the light and then "go" when it's time to change the light. If you have a competent technician, he can call his own show with a script in front of him. It's always a good idea to have more than one technician, particularly if your stage manager is in the show and can't be in the booth to call the show. In that event, one technician can call the show while the other operates the lighting board.

For a production this straightforward, it's really not necessary to have assistant stage managers (ASMs) backstage with headsets talking to the SM or technicians in the booth. However, if you feel more confident having someone overseeing the backstage area, feel free to assign a student to that post.

COSTUMES, SETS AND PROPS

This is easy. Students take care of their own costumes, prop (no more than one!) and sets which consist of a mime box or something equally portable like a pillow, a stool or even a desk if a student can be quick about getting it on or off.

You really don't need to worry about keeping track of these items. Students should design and safely store all items needed for their monologues and come to rehearsals and performances with everything they need in hand. Don't store costumes or props in your classroom. Students have lockers. Let them take ownership of this one task completely on their own. Feel free to make suggestions to students regarding their costumes, sets or props but do not take it upon yourself to locate or take care of any of these three items.

POSTERS, PROGRAMS AND TICKETS

This is something you can do or ask student volunteer to do. Come up with a design that is simple yet fun and store it on your computer to use again next year.

Assign students the task of posting posters around your school and your community (if you like) the week prior to the show. There's no need to pre-sell tickets. Sell tickets at the door. If you don't want to physically make tickets, buy a roll of drink tickets instead. Tickets should be no more than $1.00 or $2.00. Since the show should really cost you nothing to mount, any money you raise will be profit for your program. Consider selling donuts and drinks at intermission to raise even more money for your drama department.

It's important for students to see where profits go. So take whatever money you make and spend it. Purchase make-up, new props or a set of handbooks immediately after your production. Students get more excited about fundraising if they can physically see the fruits of their labour right away. It's also perfectly fine, of course, to not charge a penny and just have fun!

TAKING IT ON THE ROAD

Consider taking a selection of monologues to a local drama festival or to other schools in your area. In your guest performance space, set up one spotlight downstage centre and have students enter and exit the spot like through a revolving door without fading in between monologues. This way you don't have to worry about having a technical rehearsal at your new venue. You can simple do a Cue to Cue at the school and away you go.

Another idea is performing the monologues like you did at your school but without spotlights. Students will still **set up** and **strike** (tear down) their sets in an orderly fashion but this time it will be in clear view of the audience. You might also consider doing this at your school if you don't have access to a theatre or don't have a budget for renting lights. The effect is even more fluid when the audience appreciates how quickly and quietly students **set up** and **strike** their sets.

If you do decide to mount your monologues without stage lights you will quickly become a believer in low budget productions and it won't be long before you're mounting plays in classrooms and multipurpose rooms without stressing about spending large amounts of money on lights, costumes or sets ever again!

The Producer's Survival Kit

- A monologue evening should be short: 30 – 60 minutes with an intermission
- You will need two 2-hour rehearsals per class performing
- Have students take care of their own costumes, props and sets
- Don't charge more than $1.00 or $2.00 for admission
- Consider selling donuts and drinks at intermission to raise more money
- If you make a profit, spend it and show students what was purchased with the proceeds
- It's also fine to not charge a penny!
- Come up with a simple and fun design for your posters and tickets or have a student design them
- Encourage students to post posters in the school and community (if you like) a week prior to the performance
- If you don't have a stocked theatre or are on the road, do the show without lights or set up one spot and have students go through it like through a revolving door and without blackouts

Rehearsal #1: 2 Hours

- Number students and assign them a spotlight: spot 1 (DC), 2 (DR) or 3 (DL)
- Get students to divide themselves into 2 groups for backstage purposes
- Ask students to bring costumes and props to rehearsal and store them in their lockers for safekeeping
- Get your SM to make a list of who is where backstage and to ensure that there are 3 mime boxes on either side of the backstage area
- Explain to students that there will be a **cross fade** between

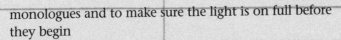

monologues and to make sure the light is on full before they begin

- Students should be in character before the lights start coming up on them and they should remain in character until they are in a complete blackout

- Ask technicians to wait for applause to die down before bringing lights up to full for the next monologue

- Do a **Cue to Cue** or **First Line Last Line** to orient and organize the actors

- Give your **director's notes** and allow time for **student notes**

- **Block** or **stage** your bows using one clean line downstage centre

- Have a dependable student in the middle of the line perform the **bowing magic trick:** right, left, bow

Rehearsal #2: 2 Hours

- Have SMs organize students backstage making sure they know their cues

- Have the lighting technicians demonstrate blackouts, cross fades and full lights

- Assign a students to do the warm-up on the day of the performance

- Do a **First Line Last Line** with the stage lights

- Ask students if they have any difficulties or concerns with the lights

- Run a full technical dress rehearsal

- Give **director's notes** and leave time for **student notes**

Lighting

- Most school theatres have access to **ellipsoidal spotlights** and **fresnel floodlights** (you'll need barn doors if you are using these)

- If you don't have a design background find someone in the school who does or pay a technician to hang and focus 9 lights – 3 for each spot area

- Illuminated areas should be tight and not overlap

- Using glow tape have technicians mark actors' **mark** with an X

- Have student technicians make a 10 count to complete each **cross fade**

- A stage manager or technician should **call the show**

- While it's not necessary to have ASMs backstage on headsets, if it makes you feel better go right ahead

Conclusion: **Get started and have fun!**

The essence of all art is to have pleasure in giving pleasure.

—Dale Carnegie

Hopefully with the lesson ideas covered in these pages, you are well on your way to exploring an exciting drama medium that is sure to engage your students and increase their self-confidence writing, directing and of course acting alone on stage.

Whether you choose to write for your students, have them write for themselves or use my scripted monologues as a starting point, I am quite certain that incorporating monologues into your curriculum will be an enriching and rewarding experience for both you and your students.

If you find yourself stuck or needing a refresher, you can always pull out your chapter-by-chapter **Survival Guides** for inspiration and clarification. Consider allowing your substitute teachers to use some of the lessons found in this book or have your class direct themselves using monologues found in chapter 5 on days that you are away or conferencing with students individually regarding their grades.

I wish you all the best in your endeavour to teach what I believe to be one of the most exciting aspects of my curriculum and something that my students eagerly anticipate on a yearly basis. Good luck and have fun!

From my classroom to yours,

Demetra Hajidiacos

Bibliography

Aristotle, *From The Poetics*, translated by L. J. Potts, *Eight Great Tragedies*. Ed. Barnet, Sylvan et al. New York: Mentor, 1985. 405-414.

Bruder, Melissa et al., *A Practical Handbook for the Actor*, New York: Vintage Books, 1986.

Halpern Charna et al., *Truth in Comedy: The Manual of Improvisation*, Colorado Springs: Meriwether Publishing Ltd., 1999.

Harrop, John and Sabin R. Epstein, *Acting with Style*, 3rd ed. Needham Heights: Allyn & Bacon, 2003.

Mamet, David, *True and False: Heresy and Common Sense for the Actor*, New York: Vintage Books, 1997.

Meisner, Sanford and Dennis Longwell, *Sanford Meisner on Acting*, New York: Vintage, 1987.

Pura, Talia, *Stages: Creative Ideas for Teaching Drama*, J. Gordon Shillingford Publishing Inc., 2002.

Wagner, Betty Jane. *Dorothy Heathcote: Drama as a Learning Medium*, Washington: National Education Association, 1985.